# PRAISE FOR SHEILA TAORMINA'S SWIM SPEED SERIES

"Sheila Taormina knows more about correct freestyle technique and mechanics than any other coach on the planet."

—STEVE HAUFLER, HEAD COACH OF THE
ORINDA COUNTRY CLUB AND ORINDA AQUATICS MASTERS

"*Swim Speed Secrets* stands alone as a gold standard for clarity, content, and results."

—TOM WHIPPLE, MS, PT, ORTHOPAEDIC PHYSICAL THERAPIST AND
AUTHOR OF *THE ENDURANCE PARADOX*

"The concept of 'holding' water and generating propulsion is fundamental to swimming performance, and Sheila's book clearly unlocks the secrets of this through words and vivid underwater photos."

—DARA TORRES, 12-TIME OLYMPIC MEDALIST

"Sheila Taormina's ideas on swimming have influenced me and my swim coaching more than anyone else. Her knowledge, experience, and enthusiasm are unmatched. *Swim Speed Secrets* is the best resource out there to help all different types of athletes improve their swim."

—SIRI LINDLEY, ITU TRIATHLON WORLD CHAMPION AND COACH TO
TRIATHLON WORLD CHAMPIONS AND OLYMPIC MEDALISTS

"Sheila T. is just 5′ 2″ but she swims like she is 6′ 2″. We still use her as a model for our swimmers today on how to swim the strokes."

—JACK BAUERLE, TEAM USA OLYMPIC SWIM COACH AND
HEAD COACH OF THE UNIVERSITY OF GEORGIA SWIM TEAM

"While I've spent the last few years training under a fantastic coach, there were still some key elements that didn't 'click' until I read [*Swim Speed Secrets*]. Having been on a plateau for some time, my swim has improved immensely within a few weeks."

—TRIEDGE.NET

"In *Swim Speed Secrets*, Sheila Taormina gives a great understanding of the art of high performance swimming. With her help, you can stop swimming for survival and start swimming like a pro."

—LAURA BENNETT, 2010 ITU #1-RANKED SWIMMER,
4-TIME ITU WORLD TRIATHLON CHAMPIONSHIP MEDALIST,
OLYMPIAN, AND 2-TIME U.S. TRIATHLON CHAMPION

"[*Swim Speed Secrets*] is a ripper! [It was] great to get a no-b.s. perspective on swimming from a champion."

"Sheila possesses a great depth of knowledge and passion about swimming that she has often shared with me and many other athletes. *Swim Speed Secrets* will be a very useful tool to anyone who wants to improve their performance in the water."

"*Swim Speed Strokes* is the best current resource on the market. It will add to the coach's knowledge base, to the coach's internalized picture of what the strokes should look like, and it will add the exact same contribution to your athletes."

"Taormina's ability to break down each stroke and rebuild it, piece by piece, all but guarantees success for swimmers and coaches in improving technique. . . . The images perfectly support her descriptions of the what, how, and why required for achieving efficiency in all aspects of all four strokes. . . . *Swim Speed Strokes* is among the best stroke technique books."

"Sheila has taken all the knowledge she has gained and refined throughout a phenomenal career and brought it to *Swim Speed Strokes*. It is a swim training bible. . . . Sheila brings her energetic, encouraging, whip-smart personality to her coaching, which is why this book is so enjoyable and educational."

"*Swim Speed Workouts* is the pool version of in-home workout videos. The cards can be used by beginning to experienced swimmers or triathletes training independently of a coach, or provide easy illustrations of drills and tubing exercises for coaches to share with their swimmers."

"Our testers, ranging from beginner to advanced swimmers, enthusiastically agreed that *Swim Speed Workouts* is a great pool-side companion. The waterproof, step-by-step workouts come in a collection of individual cards and fit seamlessly into any training program."

# SWIM SPEED SECRETS

## 2ND EDITION

# SWIM SPEED SECRETS

## 2ND EDITION

# SWIM SPEED SECRETS

## MASTER THE FREESTYLE TECHNIQUE
## USED BY THE WORLD'S FASTEST SWIMMERS

### 2ND EDITION

## SHEILA TAORMINA

Boulder, Colorado

Grid photos in Chapters 5 and 8 feature the patent-pending and trademarked STGRID™

The Halo Swim Training System™ is a trademark of Lane Gainer Company

3002 Sterling Circle, Suite 100
Boulder, CO 80301–2338 USA

VeloPress is the leading publisher of books on endurance sports. Focused on cycling, triathlon, running, swimming, and nutrition/diet, VeloPress books help athletes achieve their goals of going faster and farther. Preview books and contact us at velopress.com.

Distributed in the United States and Canada by Ingram Publisher Services

Library of Congress Cataloging-in-Publication Data
Name: Taormina, Sheila, author.
Title: Swim speed secrets: master the freestyle technique used by the
  world's fastest swimmers / Sheila Taormina.
Other titles: Call the suit
Description: Second Edition. | Boulder, Colorado: VeloPress, [2018] |
  "Originally published in 2010 as Call the Suit by Sheila Taormina"—T.p.
  verso. | "Distributed in the United States and Canada by Ingram Publisher
  Services"—T.p. verso. | Includes bibliographical references and index. |
  Identifiers: LCCN 2017053375 (print) | LCCN 2018003389 (ebook) | ISBN
  9781937716974 (eISBN) | ISBN 9781937715816 (paperback: alk. paper)
Subjects: LCSH: Swimming—Training. | Swimming—Technique.
Classification: LCC GV837.7 (ebook) | LCC GV837.7 .T364 2018 (print) | DDC
  797.21—dc23
LC record available at https://lccn.loc.gov/2017053375

This paper meets the requirements of ANSI/NISO Z39.48-1992 (Permanence of Paper).

18   19   20 / 10   9  8  7  6  5  4  3  2  1

To Greg Phill, my swim coach. You lifted the cement blocks off my shoulders before the Olympic Trials the moment you quoted John Lubbock:

*When we have done our best,*
*we should wait the result in peace.*

Also, thank you for reminding me that a couple billion people never knew when I had a bad race.

# CONTENTS

# PREFACE

When I wrote *Swim Speed Secrets* in 2011, I had one principal goal: to steer swimmers and triathletes away from excessive gliding. There was then so much talk of low stroke count that athletes were led to believe this factor was the one and only key to fast swimming. Gliding with a sleek body position became the preferred method for reaching the low stroke counts of Olympic champions. The problem was that the other half of the swimming equation—rate of turnover—was completely ignored, and athletes were not finding themselves swimming any faster.

So, I set out to introduce the "rate" side of the equation in the original edition of this book. I wanted to show athletes that once they understood the importance of rate, they would realize low stroke count is not effectively achieved by gliding but rather by properly navigating the *propulsive* phases of the stroke. The majority of my effort in the original edition was directed toward convincing readers of my rationale.

Today, in 2018, most athletes understand they must pay attention to the propulsive aspects of the stroke to achieve low stroke count while also attending to the rate side of the equation—the combination that makes for fast swimming.

I've thoroughly enjoyed watching swimmers and triathletes begin the process of adopting the very doable, although challenging, stroking mechanics of elite swimmers. Their hard work is paying off. Times are dropping and physiques are changing—telltale signs of solid mechanics.

This is exciting, but there is more. I now want to delve deeper into the stroke.

In the original edition, I did not provide enough guidance on the stroke itself. Two factors contributed to this: (1) As mentioned, my primary focus was affecting change in the swimming community's mindset; and (2) I believed that broad descriptions of the stroke were enough for readers to apply solid mechanics.

However, the more I've studied technique and worked with athletes of all levels, the more I have honed in on details that—although sometimes barely perceptible—have the power to limit performance tremendously if navigated incorrectly, or at the wrong moment, or not at all. Thus, broad descriptions are simply too vague. They leave too much room for misinterpretation, or leave out key elements altogether. If, for instance, a coach says to make a "deep catch," then how does the swimmer know what that means exactly? What is deep enough? What is too deep? Should the swimmer think about the hand, the shoulder, the elbow, or some other part of the arm when considering the depth? This uncertainty simply leaves too much to chance and too much potential on the table.

Swimming is a complex, three-dimensional sport, with depth components in addition to fore-aft and lateral components, yet there are no reference points to these dimensions in a mass of water. The movements made by swimmers, even when filmed underwater and analyzed frame by frame, are viewed against a nebulous backdrop. Couple this with the fact that swimming propulsion or speed depends on principles of physics and fluid dynamics, which require measured movements to maximize performance, and we see that coaches can end up in a quandary. They should be offering specific mechanical instruction to their athletes, but the medium in which the sport is contested is obscure, leaving them with choices for coaching instruction as vague as water itself.

Coaches have fallen into a habit of describing this complex sport in short phrases, usually in four words or less: *"rotate," "glide," "kick from the hips," "keep your head down," "reach," "pull straight back,"* and so forth. This is partly practical—swimmers get cold if they have to stand too long at the wall listening to a lengthy explanation of what to do. But it becomes far too easy to write off a slower swimmer as someone who "just doesn't have a feel for the water." If a swimmer does not improve after being instructed to "kick from the hips," for example, the instruction itself is not questioned, it is the swimmer—who either didn't start swimming at an early enough age and therefore is behind the curve and always will be, or doesn't have kinesthetic awareness, flexibility, or strength.

In this revised edition, my goal is to change that by adding the depth of guidance.

I believe elite stroking is within every athlete's grasp, but too many athletes are missing out on their potential for lack of guidance on the details. They're "making a catch," but they're doing it too late, too wide, or with improper hand speed. In the following pages, I will unpeel the deepest layers of the stroke and hone in the checklist that is required for making a great catch, as well as other phases of the stroke.

To help achieve this goal, I developed an apparatus called the STGRID™ (patent pending). The STGRID is a measurement tool that allows swim mechanics to be articulated in *measurable, definable* terms. The grid is used in conjunction with underwater cameras that film a swimmer's stroke. All movements throughout the swim stroke are measured and analyzed against the grid. Swimmers who are filmed using the STGRID can then measure their own strokes against measurements I have taken from Olympic swimmers' strokes. The elite swimmers have been measured with the STGRID on all three dimensions. While not every elite swimming stroke is exactly like another, the movements always fall within a tight set of parameters. The STGRID outlines those parameters so that aspiring swimmers can adjust their mechanics with certainty and confidence.

Those who have read the original edition of this book will recall that its theme centered on organizing the massive amount of information relating to swim technique and then focusing intently on the few vital elements of the stroke. That remains the theme in this new edition. The propulsive phases of the stroke are still where I contend we must place the majority of our focus. However, in this edition I have defined how to navigate those phases in more detail, so that athletes don't miss a critical element that can make the difference in performance.

Complementing this in-depth description of the propulsive phases of the stroke are several other related updates, including the following.

### 1. Hand Speed Change

Feel for the water is an area I've examined closely for several years. The generally accepted truth is that an athlete either "has it" or doesn't. I have never bought into that mindset. Working with hundreds of athletes over the years has led me to see that this vital element is teachable, not simply a gift of the lucky few. Feel is closely related to hand speed change throughout the stroke cycle. Not hand speed; hand speed *change.* In this edition, I teach the finer points of acceleration, namely the unique movements at the beginning of the propulsive stroke cycle that affect hand speed (hint: they do not entail a passive "gliding" motion). Once swimmers learn the details behind these movements, they will understand and "feel" the secret ingredient to achieve elite propulsion.

### 2. Oarlocks

In studying minute details of the stroke in action, I noted that some athletes employed very good mechanics but failed to effectively transfer momentum to the core. Their speed did not match their mechanics; they were slower than they should have been. This led me to the discovery of a key detail in the stroke that has never been addressed in our sport. I term it *oarlocks* and here's why it matters: unstable oarlocks diminish the effect of great mechanics. Stable oarlocks, on the other hand, reward the swimmer by maximally converting propulsive power from the limbs to the body's movement forward. In this new edition, you will learn where the oarlocks are on a swimmer and how to stabilize them. I'm extremely excited to share this crucial information with readers.

### 3. Reinforcement of Pull Path

Since the original edition of *Swim Speed Secrets* was published six years ago, an ideology that began in the early 2000s has grown in popularity—the "pull straight back" craze. I've watched with uneasiness as coaches and swimmers revile the S Pull to such an extent that they've swung the pendulum too far in the other direction. The newly chosen semantics imply that swimmers should eliminate all movement on the lateral and vertical dimensions of our three-dimensional sport. The result? Shoulder injuries are skyrocketing, and swimmers who use this path are not getting faster. While some progress has been made toward convincing athletes of the curvilinear path, the straight-back path is still too readily taught. This edition includes a section intended to redirect the pendulum, along with photos throughout of the most current freestyle Olympic medalists from Rio 2016, confirming the curvilinear path in their strokes.

### 4. New Drills

The drills in the original edition were chosen to correlate with the broad stroking guidance I gave in that book. Now that we are unveiling deeper layers of the stroke, I've selected drills that correlate with those details. Don't worry—while a few may be a little more challenging than you're accustomed to, all are very doable, and they will help you develop a championship stroke down to the last detail.

### 5. Applying Rate

Rate is a significant topic in the original edition, and here I take a more extensive look at how it is applied. Rate is not automatic; it must be trained. In the original edition, I addressed only racing rates of turnover, but in order to reach those, a swimmer must know how to apply rate of turnover in training. In this edition, I explain how that is accomplished.

### 6. The Nonvital Elements of the Stroke

Finally, while I will always believe the majority of a swimmer's focus should be on the critical underwater pull path, there are other parts of the stroke that do impact performance. In the original edition of this book I did not address those. In this edition, I dedicate a chapter to the details behind those elements, and I explain how to train them.

I'm excited to share these updates and the many discoveries I've made along the way as I've studied our amazing sport. My overarching goal with this book is the same as it has been since the first edition: to help those interested in getting faster to discover the beauty, science, and art of propulsive swimming.

Enjoy the process. Don't rush this. Swimming is a complex sport, not mastered in a day.

—**SHEILA T.**

# ACKNOWLEDGMENTS

First, thank you to my mom and dad.

Mom, for your prayers above all else—but also because, despite being a woman who says she is made of bubble gum and rubber bands, and who has never been seen getting her hair wet at a pool, and who, if I asked her today to tell me what my best 200 freestyle time was, would say something like 3 minutes because she has no clue about times, for all that, you made the perfect swimming mom. Dad, that you could sum up your life in four words and for the great swim lessons, you are my hero. I love you and miss you.

To my swim coach Greg Phill, to whom this book is dedicated. If you were taken out of the timeline of my life, the sports story would begin and end completely differently. And to your amazing wife, Jules.

To my college coaches, Jack Bauerle and Harvey Humphries at the University of Georgia. There will never be a more perfect duo. I've watched with admiration as you have built the Georgia program to number one in the country, and I know the foundation upon which it lies is authentic, balanced, and as much about life as it is about swimming. I am so thankful for all of your guidance and love.

To University of Texas coaches Eddie Reese, Chase Kreitler, Wyatt Collins, Carol Capitani, and Roric Fink, thank you for your open pool deck policy and for allowing me to film your swimmers and learn from you.

To Jack Nelson, former head coach of the Fort Lauderdale Swim Team and the only person in history to have competed as a swimmer at the Olympics (1956) and served as head coach for the USA Olympic swim team (1976). Coach, I am thankful that even a sliver of your beautiful believing mind seeped into my own. The swimming world lost one of the absolute best when we lost you.

To Jim Richardson, former head women's swim coach at the University of Michigan, thank you for making available, on a daily basis, the university's 50-meter pool before 1996. The encouragement you gave Greg and me during those days was a true gift, and your dry-erase-board lessons on swimming technique opened new levels of understanding for me.

To the athletes photographed in this book: Jack Conger, Townley Haas, Ashley Whitney, Elizabeth Beisel, Peter Vanderkaay, Allison Schmitt, Margaret Kelly, Rowdy Gaines, and Vladimir Morozov for taking time from your busy schedules to be part of this project. By sharing what you've mastered in the deep blue, you impact the lives of swimmers around the world. For that generosity you are the greatest of champions.

To Brendan Hansen, Missy Kuck, and Natasha Van Der Merwe, for your help and kind welcome to your incredible pool at the Austin Aquatics and Sports Academy for the photo shoot. More wonderful than the pool is your down-to-earth, professional, good energy.

To Kathy Coffin-Sheard, former University of Georgia teammate, coach, and treasured friend, your passion to capture the best photos is valued tremendously. And how lucky are we to have eaten at the Taco Stand three days in a row when we prepped for this project!

To Jason Hamelin at the Camera Shop, and Christopher Morey, in Traverse City, Michigan, for helping with the technical aspects of the underwater shoot.

To the sports compliance departments at the University of Georgia, University of Florida, and University of Texas for your assistance in granting permission to photograph your collegiate athletes.

To Matt Farrell at United States Swimming for tracking down historical information and Olympic swimming footage for my personal research. The timeliness with which you responded to my request was exceptional and so very much appreciated.

To Craig Askins, from Lane Gainer, for your abundant time and compassion, and for always making work "more fun than fun."

To Daniel Smith for making time in your busy schedule to work on the original edition of this book.

To Dave Tanner and Joel Stager, who are carrying the torch forward to preserve, and build upon, the work of Doc Counsilman, the greatest pioneer in the history of swimming. It was an honor to meet you and see Doc's original cameras and equipment. Also, thank you for granting permission to reprint Doc's original photos of Mike Troy and Mark Spitz.

To Bruce Wigo, executive director at the International Swimming Hall of Fame in Fort Lauderdale, for your wonderful support in tracking down historical information and for granting permission to use Johnny Weissmuller's photo. Thank you for all you do to preserve swimming history.

A special thanks to Price Fishback, my economics professor at the University of Georgia. Price, thank you for making a potentially dry subject incredibly applicable to life. Also, to my production management and business professors at the University of Georgia—Jim Cox, Gerald Horton, and James Gilbert—for your gifted teaching and genuine interest in my swimming career.

And finally, to the crew at VeloPress in Boulder—notably Dave Trendler, Ted Costantino, Renee Jardine, Kara Mannix, Andy Read, Michelle Asakawa, and Casey Blaine: From our first meeting in 2011 and throughout the years, each of you has patiently and professionally guided every project. Thank you for the opportunity to take this book to levels I would have never been able to do. Special appreciation is extended to Casey Blaine for your intuitiveness in editing the book without compromising my voice or the book's essence. You have my deepest respect and admiration for your talents, and my sincere thanks for making the work enjoyable.

Above all, a thank you to God for blessing my life with health, opportunity, the people mentioned in this book, and many others beyond.

# INTRODUCTION

How is it that elite swimmers are dizzyingly tearing apart world records while masses of triathletes, masters swimmers, and age groupers remain stumped as to why their times are barely improving, or not improving at all?

The elite swimming times are almost unreal. Consider for a moment that the women's world records are now as fast as the men's world records from the early 1970s. That means that even Mark Spitz's times from the 1972 Olympic Games are being met by the fastest women today. The 200 m freestyle is a perfect example. Today's world record for women is 1:52.98. Spitz won Olympic gold in Munich in 1:52.78.

It doesn't matter which stroke you choose, or which distance. In the 50 m freestyle, South African Jonty Skinner held the world record in 1976 with a time of 23.86. On July 29, 2017, Sarah Sjostrom of Sweden powered to a 23.67. Today's 1500 m freestyle world record for women, 15:25.48, is 27 seconds faster than the gold-medal world record–setting time for men at the 1972 Olympics.

The elite male swimmers are doing the same thing the women are doing—smashing previous marks at a rate that has left most people scratching their heads. It makes a statement made by the famous Johnny Weissmuller seem almost comical. Weissmuller, who won five Olympic gold medals in swimming at the 1924 and 1928 games, stated in his book *Swimming the American Crawl*, in the chapter "Can the Crawl Be Improved?":

*My technique has been called the "perfected" crawl stroke because it reduced water resistance to the minimum; it facilitated a method of breathing that most closely approximates the natural, involuntary method of nature; it put the body in a position to make free and unimpeded use of all its strength and power and leverage, and it got the most propulsion for the effort expended. Some say there is still room for improvement in this stroke. I do not see just where the improvement will come. (Weissmuller 1930, 45)*

Now, we have to give Weissmuller some slack for thinking the world would never improve upon what he did in the roaring '20s, because he did set 67 world records during his swimming career. In fact, he was never beaten in an official swimming race. Think about it—never beaten! If I were him, I probably would have thought I had perfected the crawl too. Also, it wasn't like he just dove

Johnny Weissmuller (aka Tarzan), swimming with the stroke that earned him five Olympic gold medals and 67 world records.

in and swam any old way he wanted. In his book, he describes—down to the smallest detail—the reasons why he used the technique he used. A great deal of thought went into it.

What was that technique? You may know it as the Tarzan drill—the drill you do in practice where you hold your head above the water. If your coach is a fun person, then he or she will insist you do the ululating Tarzan yell while you stroke (mine did).

That was Weissmuller's stroke, keeping his chest and shoulders high in the water, and the drill is called the Tarzan drill because Weissmuller became even more famous after his swimming career when he landed the role of Tarzan in the movies. Following is another excerpt from his book, in which he describes his stroke:

> *I swim with my chest and shoulders high in the water. This enables me to hydroplane, like a speedboat, reducing resistance to a minimum. I swim higher in the water than anybody ever did before, higher than anybody else does to this day. . . . The height of my chest enables me to arch my back, avoiding the strain of the swayback position which many have to take in order to get the face out of the water for inhaling. The high chest and shoulders and the arch of the back throw my feet lower in the water, where they maintain traction at all times. (Weissmuller 1930, 20)*

Weissmuller wrote that he also believed the hips should stay flat, because, as he explains, if the hips roll, then the corresponding arm and shoulder dip lower in the water, thus causing resistance.

Today's freestyle swim technique we know to be the exact opposite. The only people holding their heads above water are people who do not want to get their hair wet, like my mom, and using the hips as part of the stroke is most certainly on everyone's radar.

So, are you wondering where I'm going with this?

If you think we are headed for a discussion on reducing resistance, then guess again. Rather, I am going to use Weissmuller and a number of other swimmers who have reigned as champions in the pool for the past five decades to present a picture of swimming that is long overdue—a picture that answers a great many questions.

To begin painting this picture, let me set the scene with the following shocking information: Even though Weissmuller's times have long been shattered (his 100 m freestyle world record was first broken in 1934), his fastest 100 m freestyle still beats 95 percent of triathletes (even the top professionals), 95 percent of masters swimmers, and 95 percent of age-group swimmers today. It is indeed strange commentary that Weissmuller would beat just about every person reading this book.

Let's look at his times: In February 1924, Weissmuller swam a 57.4 in the 100 m freestyle (long course meters). Sure, the world record now is 46.91, set by Cesar Cielo of Brazil (2009 World Championships), and the women's world record is 51.71 (Sarah Sjostrom of Sweden, 2017 World Championships), but how many of you who are reading this book would think you were the cat's meow for going a time like Weissmuller's?

And it wasn't just the short races in which Weissmuller set world records. He also owned the 400 m and 800 m freestyle records: 4:57.0 in the 400, set in 1923, and 10:22.2 in the 800, set in 1927. Although not nearly as impressive as his 100 m freestyle time, those distance event times would still, even today, place him in the lead, or very near the lead, at any triathlon event going into T-1 (Transition 1, which is triathlon talk for the changeover from the swim to the bike).

I realize that Weissmuller's times may not impress all of you in the swimming world today, especially his 400 and 800 times (Weissmuller was definitely more of a sprinter than a distance swimmer), which means at this point some of you may think this book is too elementary. It may appear that I am going to address only the crowd that needs to catch up with swimming times that were posted almost 100 years ago. Don't close the book so fast. This book is invaluable for a swimmer with national times, or the coach of a swimmer with those times, because it is as much about thought processes as it is about swim technique. You may be on the verge of cracking into the very top of the elite ranks but wonder how you are going to climb the next rung of the ladder. The insights provided in this book will help you do that.

The reason many of us have been stumped about how to make improvements in our times, or how to reach the next level, is not for lack of information but rather for lack of organization of the information. A fair number of swimmers work on things that have minimal to zero impact on their times, because they were never accurately told what is most important and which things must be developed first. This book will change that.

You should know why you do what you do at every moment when you are working on technique or training.

I have a mantra, in sport and in life, that is about taking charge. It is "call the suit." In my favorite card game, Euchre, each player is given the opportunity at various times during the game to call the suit that will be "trump" (most pow-

USA Olympic Team Members Allison Schmitt and Sheila Taormina showing that fast swimming isn't just about wingspan!

erful). Players must look at the hands they were dealt and on their turn make a decision about whether to take charge of the play of the game or pass the opportunity to the next player, their competitor. I always encourage people to "call the suit!" Be bold. Understand what you have in your hand, and then make an informed decision on how best to play the game from there.

We are seldom coached on how to do this in our lives. My goal is to show the thought process that will develop this in your swimming, and it will actually be a launching pad for you to apply it to other areas of your life as well.

I've limited the book to the discussion of one stroke, freestyle, because it is the stroke that I know inside and out. It is the stroke that took me to the Olympics four times. I studied it, I spent endless moments thinking about it in the pool, and I got to know it. I am a fraction of an inch over 5 foot 2 inches in height, so my wingspan was not what put me on the Olympic team—it was the understanding of how to take information and make it work.

If you are new to swimming, please do not be intimidated by this book. The principles are simple. You will understand everything, and it will help you see the path to your goals.

Last, and perhaps most important, let's keep everything in perspective: We are not solving any world crisis here. Let's have fun. I am almost certain that if I had had to give up coffee in order to do sports, then I probably would have given up sports. (OK, I'm joking . . . maybe.) Make sure to read the dedication if you need additional perspective, and let's move forward with answering the question from the beginning of this introduction.

Here's wishing you joy on your journey to understanding the beautiful sport of swimming.

# 1

# THE PARETO PRINCIPLE

## APPLYING THE 80/20 RULE IN THE POOL

**SWIMMING IS AN INCREDIBLY DYNAMIC SPORT.** Every part of your body is doing something all of the time when you swim competitively. Even the head, which stays neutral and steady, needs to be turned to take a breath. It can be an information-management nightmare, not only for beginners trying to learn the sport but also for experienced swimmers who are at a loss to identify exactly what they are missing that will take them to the next level.

In case you have never thought about the complexity of the task, let's contrast swimming with other sports that are less dynamic in terms of technique. The examples that follow are two disciplines with which I am very familiar, having experienced both on the Olympic stage.

**Pistol shooting.** There are great challenges in this sport (remaining focused and calm under pressure, for example), but the technique is very static. A pistol shooter methodically progresses through each step in the process, focusing on one element of the sequence at a time, until the shot is fired. Therefore, the training of shooting technique is not overwhelming.

Remaining composed under competition pressure? That is a completely different story, for another book.

**Cycling.** This sport falls in the middle of the static-dynamic spectrum. While the legs are dynamically powering the pedal stroke, the upper body is quite still. Anytime a cyclist chooses to focus on technique—a smoother pedal stroke, for example—she needs only to focus on the lower half of the body. Therefore, the learning curve and application of technique are quite manageable. The keys to success for this sport are as difficult as in any other sport, but mentally managing technique is not one of them.

Managing technique in swimming, compared with these other sports, is a beast of a task. During any given length of the pool, a swimmer may choose to perfect one of many elements of the stroke. While working on that one element, the swimmer must also consider how to make it work synchronously with the other parts of the stroke. Then throw in the fact that this is managed within a medium that is not natural to humans—water—and the recipe can be overwhelming. My guess is that because of all this, a high percentage of the people who are reading this book are frustrated as to why their swimming times have not improved after all the hours they have spent in the pool. I hear you. I went through the same frustrations with fencing when learning that for the pentathlon.

Fencing, like swimming, is incredibly dynamic. Every body part is doing something all the time, even down to the fingers that hold the grip, and the timing of every body part is crucial. Although the sport is contested in a natural environment for the athlete—land—its true complexity is revealed when the athlete is faced with another human being on the other side of the competition strip thwarting every attempted move. During the years I tried to grasp each detail of fencing technique, from age 36 to 39, my coaches continually yelled, in thick Eastern European accents, "Why you do that?" If I was thinking about my arm, then my legs were messing up; if I was thinking about my footwork, then I missed the timing. One coach would tell me to lean forward more, and another coach would say to stand up more. There was so much to think about simultaneously that I didn't know where to start, nor did I know which coach to trust.

Believe me, I empathize with anyone learning the sport of swimming and with those who have been at it for a while but have seen no improvement in performance. I also relate to the huge population of coaches and swimmers who have experienced a fair amount of success in swimming but who want to know what it takes to reach the next level, or perhaps to crack the elite ranks one day.

The good news is, while I cannot help you with your fencing, I can definitely help with your swimming. What we have to do is begin sorting and organizing the information.

## EMPLOYING THE PARETO PRINCIPLE

Because swimming is so dynamic, the only way to get a solid grip on where to start is to manage all the information. The best way I know of sorting information is to employ the Pareto principle, also known as the 80/20 rule. The Pareto principle is not a hard-and-fast rule; rather, it is applied as a rule of thumb, most commonly in arenas such as business and science. When I first learned about it in 1993, I saw immediately how it could be a tool for sports. I applied it to my swimming before the 1996 Olympics and to every sport I have done since.

Vilfredo Pareto was an Italian economist who, in the early 1900s, took note that approximately 80 percent of the wealth in his country belonged to 20 percent of the people. After his notation, others realized that you could apply this 80/20 concept to many aspects of life. In business, a salesperson might note that 80 percent of sales come from 20 percent of clients, or that 80 percent of problems

Vilfredo Pareto, Italian industrialist, economist, and philosopher come from 20 percent of clients. In our personal lives, we may note that we spend 80 percent of our time with 20 percent of our acquaintances, and so on.

The Pareto principle is also known as the law of the vital few. It says that there are a few aspects (20 percent) of anything we do that have the greatest impact (80 percent) on what we are trying to accomplish. The other 80 percent of things, added together, do not have nearly the same impact as those vital few.

In a sport, if we can identify the vital few things that give the greatest impact, then we are much better equipped to design an effective plan that brings us closer to our goal. We do not ignore the other 80 percent of things that give us some return; we simply know where they fall in the list of priorities.

In this book, I am going to show you the vital few items of swimming technique. They are extremely important. They give us 80 percent of what we need to be a fast swimmer. While the full scope of the freestyle stroke is addressed in this book, remember that developing the vital few pays the biggest dividends (or, put another way, is a showstopper if not present in your stroke).

## TECHNIQUE IS 80 PERCENT OF SWIMMING

When you are swimming up and down the pool, you are usually alone with your own thoughts. Coaches stand over your lane every once in a while, but for the most part you are in charge of whether you are thinking about technique or what's for dinner.

I have to drive home the point that technique is, by far, the most important aspect of swimming. There is no reason why we cannot apply the 80/20 rule here: Technique is 80 percent of swimming when lined up next to strength, conditioning, or the size of a swimmer.

Conditioning and strength are very important in swimming, but they will not get you far without good technique. Ask the strongest football player you know to swim one length of the pool. If he has not learned technique, then he will look like a drowning rat in the water, and it is not because his muscles are weighing him down. It is the same with conditioning. You could ask a sub-2:40 marathoner to swim, and if she does not know swim technique, then all the conditioning in the world will not help. This is one of the scenarios where the vital elements are important because they are the foundation upon which the other elements rely. Technique takes the 80 percent prize because without it strength and conditioning mean nothing. That being said, once we have developed a solid technique the ratios change, and our physical training kicks in much more.

I see too many athletes allowing their strokes to fall apart when they tire at practice. Or, worse, I see people choosing to forgo technique altogether and thrash at the water in order to keep up with their lane mates. The only way you will benefit from reading this book is if you commit to making the vital elements of swim technique a priority.

In fact, my goal is to get you so excited about your understanding of swimming technique after reading this book that you actually become addicted to making that your focus during practice. Then, once you're on a good roll with technique, the training, conditioning, and strength become fascinating and much more meaningful. You are probably getting antsy by now to find out which are the vital few elements and may want to skip ahead to find them. Don't do that just yet. We have to go over the big-picture understanding of swimming first. After that, we will begin to name the vital few and explain how to develop them.

So, in honor of Vilfredo, brew up a good Italian-roast espresso, take a comfortable seat, and enjoy the next few chapters.

# 2

# THE BIG PICTURE

## UNDERSTANDING THE SWIMMING EQUATION

**IN THIS CHAPTER YOU WILL BE PRESENTED** with the big-picture view of swimming. Once you understand the big picture, the details of technique will begin to make much more sense. You will be able to answer many of the questions about technique for yourself, and your swimming will go to a whole new level. You will have confidence, and the laps up and down the pool will begin to mean something. The best part is how simple it all is.

First, let's set the stage (see Figure 2.1): You are going to push off the wall and swim 25 meters. We will assume that you begin the 25-meter swim with a good underwater streamline—a contoured body position used by swimmers to

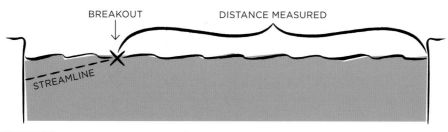

**FIGURE 2.1**

reduce water resistance after diving into a pool or pushing off a wall. The vast majority of elite competitive swimmers employ an underwater streamline for 2–3 seconds before surfacing to begin stroking.

Now you are on the surface swimming.

Only two things affect the time it takes you to get from your breakout (the moment a swimmer surfaces and begins stroking) to the end of the pool. These two factors are not the "vital few" elements from our Pareto principle discussion; we will get to those soon. However, these two key factors make up the swimming equation that frames the big picture:

- The number of strokes you take to get across the pool
- The rate at which you take those strokes (turnover)

## NUMBER OF STROKES AND RATE

Let's say that it takes you 10 strokes (full arm cycles) to get to the end of the pool. Let's also say it takes you 1 second per stroke.

If you multiply the number of strokes by the rate at which you take those strokes, then you get your time. Here is what it looks like in equation form:

**(Number of Strokes) × (Rate of Turnover) = Time (in seconds)**

Let's insert the numbers from our example:

**10 strokes × 1 second/stroke = 10 seconds**

Number of Strokes    Rate of Turnover    Time

Mathematically it looks like this (remember from math class, we cross out the "strokes" in our equation):

$$10 \text{ strokes} \times \frac{1 \text{ second}}{\text{stroke}} = 10 \text{ seconds}$$

One stroke is a full arm cycle. In other words, one stroke is from the point when one arm enters the water until that same arm enters the water again. A different way to count strokes is to count "one" when the right arm goes in and then "two" when the left arm goes in, and so on. Both methods of counting are equally acceptable, but in this book stroke counts refer to full cycles.

That's it. There is the big picture. You can only get faster in swimming in one of two ways:

- Reduce the number of strokes you take.
- Turn over the strokes more quickly.

You just learned what I learned at age 25. I had competed in two Olympic Trials (1988 and 1992) before I learned this simple equation. A new level of understanding opened up for me, and this knowledge helped me make my first Olympic team in 1996. You might be tempted to take just this one thing and run with it (and you could), but while it is true that only two factors affect our swimming time, many things affect those two factors. Still, we are on our way. We now have the big picture around which we can frame the details of technique. So remember, when you read something about swim technique, or if your coach tells you to change your stroke, ask yourself how it will influence either the number of strokes you take or the rate at which you take them.

## THE SWIMMING EQUATION IN PRACTICE

Let's look at the equation more closely and take note of how the two factors work in a real-life situation.

To reduce our time in swimming, the two factors must be lowered. We can either lower one or the other, or lower both. The tricky part is that sometimes we get excited that we reduced one, but we forget to check how the other was affected.

The two factors are not always independent of each other. Sometimes the steps we take to reduce one factor end up increasing the other. The best way to explain this is to give two examples. (Note: The numbers I am using in these examples are chosen for the sake of simplicity. Chapter 8 examines the actual stroke counts and rate numbers we see in the top swimmers.)

## EXAMPLE 1: REDUCING STROKES

A weekend swimming clinic is coming to town. It is marketed as holding the key to unleashing your swimming potential. At the clinic, swimmers are told that taking fewer strokes is better. The focus is entirely on reducing the number of strokes to get across the pool. From our equation, we know this is a good thing. However, at this clinic, the swimmers are not told about the other half of the equation.

All weekend, the participants are in the water—reaching, extending, and gliding out front. They look beautiful and smooth.

The athletes get excited about having reduced their number of strokes from 10 down to 8. They probably raised their hands to tell the coach the good news, and the coach probably high-fived them. But, here is the problem: The coach never told them about rate. No one timed their turnover. Now, instead of taking 1 second per stroke, the swimmers are taking 1.5 seconds per stroke, because they are gliding out front so long on every stroke.

By the end of the clinic, their equation looks like this:

$$8 \text{ strokes} \times \frac{1.5 \text{ seconds}}{\text{stroke}} = 12 \text{ seconds}$$

Yikes! They became slower. They left the clinic thinking they had become faster, but the opposite was true. And the reason they got slower was that they were taught only half the equation and led to believe they could improve their swimming by focusing only on reducing their number of strokes.

They may not realize this for a while. In fact, many of them may never quite understand, instead always wondering what they did wrong. I hope this book gets into the hands of everyone who has experienced that disappointment, because I want to tell them that they did nothing wrong. The problem was that they were never given the full picture. They were only given half the equation and thought that was all they needed to be on their way to swimming stardom.

The bottom line is that you cannot improve your swimming by focusing only on the number-of-strokes side of the equation through gliding out front. That is not what competitive swimmers do to improve their swim times.

That said, gliding does serve one particular group of swimmers quite well. It serves the swimmer who would like to enjoy the sport simply for exercise or is learning to swim just to survive through a triathlon or, as a friend of mine once put it, in case your boat sinks. In other words, anyone who is not focused on time and who merely wants the enjoyment of being able to swim (or is a survivalist) will benefit wonderfully from stretching out his or her stroke. It is less taxing, is simple to do, and provides a healthy, low-impact way to exercise.

However, if you are a swimmer who wants to be competitive, then you have to stay with me for a while longer to find out how to reduce the number of strokes you take without adversely affecting your rate.

## EXAMPLE 2: REDUCING RATE

For this example, let's imagine a completely different scenario. You are at an age-group swim meet, and the adorable 8 and unders are on the blocks for the 25-yard freestyle. Their goggles are on crooked, their suits are too big for them, and they are ready to jump in and give it their all. They have so much energy stored up that they are like wind-up toys, which is exactly what they look like when they race down the pool. Their arms spin at warp speed. They take about a million strokes to get to the other end. It is the cutest thing ever!

Here is what their equation looks like:

$$15 \text{ strokes} \times \frac{0.8 \text{ seconds}}{\text{stroke}} = 12 \text{ seconds}$$

The great effort that was just put forth ends up not paying off. The time is slower. Even though the rate side of the equation was reduced, the number of strokes went up significantly, because the arms never "held" the water. This scenario can be likened to a car's wheels spinning on ice.

Most people reading this book will fall into the category of Example 1, but understanding what is going on in Example 2 is important. Learning to "hold" the water is critical. If you are paying close attention to words, then *critical* is your clue that we are getting closer to discussing the 20 percent of stroke elements that take us 80 percent of the way to optimizing both factors in our equation.

# 3

# THE VITAL ELEMENT
## A CASE TO PROVE IT

**NOW THAT YOU UNDERSTAND THE SWIMMING EQUATION** and the fact that both the number of strokes and the rate of turnover are important, we are ready to move on to what I consider the vital elements in swimming. To kick off, we need to look at the topic of water, and understand the options before us. Water is a fascinating medium, midway between air and a solid object. Picture yourself trying to grab air. You cannot hold it. You cannot pull yourself forward. Now, picture yourself holding onto a solid object that is anchored in the ground, like a signpost. If you hold the post with your hand, you can pull your body forward. Your hand stays locked on the post, and your body moves in the direction you pulled.

Water has more substance (viscosity or density) than air but is not as solid as an object that is anchored. The especially interesting part about water is that, depending on what we do, it can be manipulated in different ways. We can apply pressure to it and feel its mass resist us, or we can slip through it like a seal.

As swimmers, we want to work with the water in both of those ways simultaneously. Swimming is a three-dimensional sport. We have a depth component in addition to the lateral and forward/backward components. It is this depth component that makes swimming different from other sports. Two beautiful dynamics are going on at the same time. One dynamic is taking place on the surface of the water, and the other is taking place deeper, where the arm is pulling.

## FEELING THE WATER'S RESISTANCE

Let's look first at what takes place deep in the water, where the arm is pulling. Here we want to work with the water to feel its resistance.

If you have ever heard someone say, "Wow, she has a great feel for the water" or "Look at the hold he has on the water," then what you were hearing was that the swimmer was doing a great job of using the water's mass to generate propulsion. From the pool deck it may look like the swimmer is moving effortlessly, but in reality there is a lot of work going on beneath the surface. The hand and arm seek the water's resistance rather than allowing it to slip past (see Figure 3.1).

For all of the out-of-date elements Johnny Weissmuller wrote about in *Swimming the American Crawl,* such as keeping the chest and shoulders high and not using his hips, he was way ahead of his time when it came to the concept of feeling the water beneath him. This 1920s Olympian wrote the following beautiful description: "Water is elusive, but you can get 'hold' of it if you know how to go after it" (Weissmuller 1930, 62).

Another phrase he used to convey the job of holding water was "purchase power." He described how his arm would "feel for the purchase" of the water. Today we use the term "catch." The catch is essentially the very first moment that we get our hold, or feel, for the water. It happens out front. After our hand/arm enters the water and extends, we grab it, "catch it," "purchase it," and then stay on it—hold it.

There are a number of ways to describe the concepts of "catching" and "holding" the water. A coach once told me to envision a brick wall underneath me.

**FIGURE 3.1** Allison Schmitt, 2012 Olympic gold medalist, catches the water below while reducing resistance at the surface.

He said, "Grab a hold of it, lock on, and pull your body over the wall." That vision worked for me. Some coaches, however, believe this is a misrepresentation of what is going on under the water. Cecil Colwin, legendary Australian swimming coach and author of a number of insightful books on technique and training, described it this way in *Breakthrough Swimming*:

> *To convey the concept of a force acting on a mass of water, the act of propulsion has been variously described as feeling for undisturbed water, anchoring the hand on a fixed spot in the water and pulling the body past it. . . . These descriptions, strictly speaking, are inappropriate because the propulsive force is not applied against a solid or rigid resistance. Coaches should use carefully chosen words when instructing a swimmer. (Colwin 2002, 109)*

Colwin is correct; words should be chosen carefully. Water indeed is not a rigid substance. Semantics are important, but keep in mind that a particular description may register for one person while another description turns on the light for someone else. I benefited tremendously from picturing a wall beneath me. We have more to discuss about this concept of the "feel" and "hold" of the "elusive water," Colwin's ideas included, but for now the main take-away is that there is an application of force we must place against the water with our pulling arm.

## REDUCING RESISTANCE

While the "hold" is taking place below us, our relationship with the water is completely different on the surface. The head, shoulders, torso, hips, and legs should slip through the water. We do not want to feel the water in front of us resist us. We have to move through it.

This is the part of swimming where we have been taught to think about body position and roll, head position, and any other technique that reduces resistance. While definitely aspects of swimming that require our attention, these techniques are purposefully rated secondary in this book. They are already being thoroughly discussed, and with too much emphasis, elsewhere. They are such hot topics that they are smothering any discussion of what really makes a swimmer competitive—the pull underneath.

## THE VITAL ELEMENT REVEALED

There, the cat's out of the bag! Competitive swimming is far more about the pull than it is about body or head position. Take a sip of that Italian-roast coffee I hope you're drinking, and offer a toast to Pareto, because we have just revealed 80 percent of swimming! If you don't believe me, then go to a beach and watch the sunbathers wade into the water and proceed to float on their backs, soaking in the warm sun. They have a wonderful body position on top of the water—as good as I did when I swam at the Olympics. The kicker is that they are not getting anywhere. Remember, swimmers need to move forward.

Now, don't misunderstand. Body position is definitely something that the top swimmers understand and try to perfect. Scientists, coaches, and swimsuit manufacturers all study the flow of water over and around the body, so I am not saying that this is not a factor in swimming. What I am saying is that the most successful swimmers have worked to develop something that is far more vital: the pull. The only reason their work on body position means anything is because these swimmers are already tearing up the pool with an incredible pull.

## PULL VERSUS BODY POSITION

I can sense the doubt from a few of you. You are just like a good friend of mine who is a top triathlete in his age group. He has been a student of the "glide like a fish theory" for a number of years and is very protective of it. He and I had a conversation during which he described a swim clinic he attended over a decade ago. By the end of the two-day clinic he was so convinced that swimming started and ended with body-position considerations only, that he actually believed the pull under the water was a fixed force. In other words, he believed that no matter what position he held his arm in, he was applying the same force, so to him the pull was a moot point. At the clinic, there was no discussion about the underwater pull. My friend believed his only potential for improvement was to reduce resistance or, as he put it, "to get his entire body to go through as narrow a tube as possible."

He said he had been working on this for more than a decade. When I asked him if he had become faster, he admitted, "Well, no." The look I gave him said it all: You are one of the most intelligent guys I know, so how in the world did you not realize something was wrong?

Books on the market today include every detail you would want to know about the swim stroke. They are full of great information, but none of them organizes the information to reveal the vital few. People who read those books are naturally going to gravitate to the aspects of technique that are most simple to apply. However, those aspects will not be beneficial if you lack the foundation of a solid pull.

I realize that I have to back up this claim, so let's get to that now. The following reasons explain why the pull is the vital factor and why body position is not.

## REASON 1: COMMON DENOMINATOR AMONG THE WORLD'S BEST SWIMMERS

The pull is what the best swimmers have in common. When I studied underwater video and photos of the greatest swimmers throughout the past five decades, I noticed that the critical position of the arm under the water was virtually the same.

The world-record holders of the 1960s, 1970s, and 1980s were using the same crucial elements of the pull as the fastest swimmers do today. This, in and of itself, does not prove a thing. However, when combined with the fact that every triathlete and swimmer I know who struggles with going fast in the water is employing fantastic body-position technique yet none of the critical elements of the underwater pull, some conclusions can be made.

Why do we not see every serious swimmer and triathlete churning out a 57.4 in the 100 m freestyle like Johnny Weissmuller did? It is because Weissmuller knew how to "purchase" the water, as he said, and many athletes today have never given that a thought. Everyone is busy trying to get through that narrow tube my friend described. It is time to take a lesson from Weissmuller and figure out how to get ahold of the "elusive" and move forward.

If Weissmuller's time is not fast enough for you, then I'll step it up a notch. Let's look at Mark Spitz. He swam a 1:52 in the 200 m freestyle (long course) at the 1972 Munich Olympics. At the time, he was lugging around a big mustache and swimming in a nylon suit that is nothing like the space-age suits worn today. The pike dive, which essentially stops a swimmer dead in the water, was the rage, and there was no talk about "pressing the T" and "swimming downhill."

I could go on about how pool technology has improved and goggles were not allowed in 1972 and a number of other things, but hopefully the point has been made: You can try to get streamlined and reduce resistance all you want, but if you don't know how to hold the water beneath you and pull properly, then

Spitz is going to crush you with his big, hairy mustache in tow, and Weissmuller is going to embarrass you even more as he sings his Tarzan song and strokes to victory with a technique that would mortify students and coaches of the "body position and glide" school.

## REASON 2: THE LAW OF DIMINISHING RETURNS

This law is one of the most famous in all of economics (sorry, Pareto). It states that we will get less and less extra output when adding additional doses of an input while holding other inputs fixed. This law relates to our swimming situation in that once a swimmer is horizontal in the water, then we will get less and less extra output (i.e., faster swimming):

- When we add additional doses of an input (i.e., trying to get more horizontal in the water)
- While holding other inputs fixed (i.e., keeping the crummy pull fixed).

This is exactly what is happening in the triathlon world and in much of the swimming world. Around 95 percent of the swimmers and triathletes I know (professionals included) are showing up to practice and working on diminishing returns.

How can this be? Why do so many people continue to work on elements of stroke technique that don't give them significant returns while completely ignoring the vital aspects? Though I can't be certain, I have a good guess as to how the story panned out.

Top swimmers and coaches have always searched for ways to get faster. Races are won and lost in increments of hundredths of seconds, so part of the study of swimming throughout the years has been to identify areas in which any gain, no matter how small, can be made. In the 1990s body position became the new rage. I remember it clearly. I was swimming in Michigan with the Clarenceville Swim Club and rumor made its way across the country that a man named Bill Boomer was working with the Stanford swimmers on how to use the body core to improve swimming power, efficiency, and speed. It was mysterious to me; phrases such as "pressing the T" were being thrown around, and I had no idea what they meant. I just knew it was big stuff if Stanford was buying into it. Luckily, I was busy working on other glaring weaknesses, like not wimping out when my coach told me to swim 6 × 100 on 8:00 all out.

Anyway, an interesting thing happened at that time. While body-core concepts were being touted in the collegiate and club swimming world, a need, and thus a new market opportunity, for swim instruction was simultaneously growing within the triathlon and swimming world. Swim clinics began to sprout up around the country, and their focus was this new and exciting revelation about the body core and how to apply it to improve speed and power. Masters swimmers and triathletes signed up in droves, believing they were finally being handed the ticket to swimming prowess. Every other element of swim technique was virtually ignored—particularly the most vital one: the pull.

New information naturally breeds a flurry of enthusiasm. At some point, though, a leader must emerge to tame the excitement. A level-headed analysis requires that we understand how new information fits within the overall scope of our mission. Businesses and other types of organizations create mission statements and vision statements exactly for this reason—to guide decision-making and to be constantly reminded of the core of their existence. Otherwise, it is very easy to go astray, chasing rabbits. We have a limited amount of time, energy, and resources, so the majority of our work efforts had better be spent on activities that impact the bottom line.

This point was driven home in 2001 while I was touring a Mrs. T's Pierogies manufacturing plant in Pennsylvania. As I stood in awe, witnessing thousands of pierogies streaming down the conveyer belt, I shouted over the noise of the machines to the president of the company, who was standing nearby, "This is a lot of pierogies! Do you make anything other than pierogies?"

His response, shouting back, was, "Well, one time we tried to make ravioli . . . but then we realized after a little while that we are just really good at making pierogies."

Mrs. T's knew the key to its success. The company tried something new, but it saw that the ravioli business was diverting too much energy and resources away from what made it successful.

With regard to your swimming, I assume that your vision or mission is to move forward, and at a pretty good clip at that. The core of your existence, if you are to be competitive in the sport, is time (remember, number of strokes × rate of turnover, from Chapter 2). Be careful not to chase rabbits (such as pursuing a reduction in stroke count without checking how it affects your time). Every choice you make needs to effectively support your vision.

The question then becomes, how do we know when new information supports our mission or diverts resources away from it? The answer: We will not know, or at minimum we will be taking a wild guess, unless we delve deeper into understanding all that is involved in the making of something. In other words, for you to take charge of your swimming goals and ensure that your efforts in the pool provide a certain level of return (rather than diminishing returns), you must understand what goes into the making of an authentic competitive swimmer. You must become what one of my favorite authors, Matthew B. Crawford, in his book *Shop Class as Soulcraft*, calls a "craftsperson." Crawford, a motorcycle mechanic with a PhD in political philosophy, sways the reader to value the skills of the manual trades worker (i.e., plumber, electrician, mechanic) as much as the "soft-knowledge" skills of business executives. Among his many arguments—not the least of which is that the skills of the manual trades cannot be outsourced to other countries and will never become obsolete—is that a craftsperson, because of his or her understanding of the production narrative (the details that go into the making of something), does not discard things that are perfectly serviceable in a relentless pursuit of the new.

In swimming, what if we all became craftspeople? If we really knew what went into the making of a fast swimmer—in other words, our "production narrative"—then our laps up and down the pool could be designed to effectively support any goal. We would know which elements of stroke technique most impact the bottom line and which ones have minimal effect.

I want to show you the real picture of what the fastest swimmers do. I will endeavor to show you in upcoming chapters the production narrative so that your efforts in the pool provide you with a significant return rather than a diminishing return.

## REASON 3: THE THEORETICAL SQUARE LAW

The implications of the theoretical square law are found in many textbooks on swimming. The most practical explanation is found in *The Science of Swimming,* by James Counsilman:

> *The Theoretical Square Law: The resistance a body creates in water (or any fluid or gas) varies approximately with the square of its velocity. To illustrate this fact, let us use an airplane going 100 mph and say that it creates 10,000 pounds of resistance. When the airplane doubles its speed to 200 mph, it does not simply double its resistance; rather, the resistance increases by four times, or to 40,000 pounds. If the plane increases its speed to 300 mph, it now increases its resistance by nine times. This law also applies to the swimmer's speed and resistance in the water. (Counsilman 1968, 16–17)*

The important word here is "square." Remember from math class that squared means "to the second power." This is not the same as doubling. The theoretical square law is important to understand with regard to swimming because it tells us that as we increase our speed, the resistance grows at an *exponential rate,* not simply at a rate proportional to the increase in speed.

This means that when a swimmer is traveling at faster speeds, resistance becomes more of an issue. We have the quintessential chicken-and-egg question here: Which comes first, forward propulsion or reducing resistance? The answer is provided by the theoretical square law: Moving forward comes first. Only when we are traveling at greater speeds does resistance become an exponentially concerning factor.

Think about the Tour de France. When does the peloton break up and stay broken up? Not on the flat sections where the speed is fast, but rather in the mountains where the speed is slower. If we think about the theoretical square law in this situation, it makes perfect sense. The cyclists leading the pack on the flat sections are traveling upward of 30 miles per hour in many places, and the resistance for them is massive. Every other cyclist can tuck behind the leaders and dodge the resistance. Once the mountains appear and the speeds slow down, however, the resistance for the leaders is much less. This is when strength becomes important, and when we see the best cyclists shine. Drafting no longer provides much advantage: The steeper the incline, the slower the speed, and the slower the speed, the less resistance the lead cyclists are facing (exponentially!). In the mountains, every cyclist is riding on a more level playing field, so to speak.

Going back to the theoretical square law as it applies to swimming: Reducing resistance becomes a relevant concern only if we are moving forward.

The leaders in the cycling pack face resistance, while the peloton tucks behind.

Swimmers should invest their energy, focus, and time on developing elements of the stroke that first and foremost provide the propulsive forces. You should spend 80 percent of your time working on the elements of technique that generate velocity. The top swimmers are doing this.

## STILL SOME SKEPTICS?

No way! Some of you are still skeptical? Seriously? Even though we just finished talking about the theoretical square law and the law of diminishing returns, pierogies, and everything else? Fine, then: I am totally game for this drag-'em-down, knock-'em-out boxing match. Here are a few additional arguments to back up my claim that the pull is the most vital part of swimming.

### FIRST, THE ONE-TWO COMBO

Our pull dictates both the number of strokes we take and the rate at which we take those strokes. No other part of swimming has a greater impact on those two factors.

### NEXT, A LIGHT JAB

Think about the physical attributes of great swimmers. What is the most distinctive look of their bodies? It is the shoulders and the lat muscles; they have broad shoulders and distinctive V-shaped bodies, right? Well, common sense would tell us that if swimmers are meant to be most concerned with reducing resistance, then they should taper down those shoulders and lats a bit. Also, how did they get that look in the first place? Something tells me they did not get it from doing six-count extension and hip-rotation drills all day long.

### THIRD, I'VE GOT MY OPPONENT AGAINST THE ROPES

You can get a great body position very quickly and with next to no physical effort. Remember those beachgoers floating on the water? Believe me, those vacationers are not stressing out trying to get that body position as they float on the water. In fact, most swimmers I have seen, whether age groupers, masters swimmers, or triathletes, have body positions worthy of an Olympic athlete. If the critical aspect of swimming fast pertained primarily to body position, then the whole world would be streaming through the water at great speeds, because everyone could develop it quickly and with little effort.

## LAST, WATCH OUT, HERE COMES THE LEFT HOOK

If you are a triathlete, masters swimmer, or age grouper who has worked excessively on body position, and not on the pull, then I am willing to guess that your warm-up speed in practice is not much different from your main set speed. I see it all the time, especially in adults. They dive in for a warm-up and go a 1:27 on their first 100 yards. Then when the main set comes along, and they are supposed to be working hard at their repeat 100s, they crank out 1:30s. Ouch. That is not how it is supposed to work.

Great swimmers have a variety of speeds, including warm-up speeds, aerobic training speeds, threshold speeds, lactate speeds, and pure sprint speeds. They are able to vary their speed based on how much force they choose to put into their propulsion; it is not based on whether they choose to improve their body position on the threshold set more than on the warm-up.

This argument is winding down, but I still see one last bit of fight left in my skeptical opponent. I hear the rebuttal: "Come on! We cannot expect someone to swim with their feet dragging on the bottom of the pool."

I say, fair enough. I'll concede that no one should have to struggle through the water vertically (nor should any observer have to suffer through watching that), but generating propulsion gets the legs up instantly. (Very new beginners, see the sidebar on p. 26.)

The last point from my opponent is that the pull is too advanced to explain to new swimmers. I would say, "Oh, please let me stand in the room when you tell them that."

## THE PULL: GOOD NEWS AND BAD NEWS

I only have a little bit of bad news: The pull definitely takes more effort and time, and is more difficult to learn than any other aspect of swimming; this is partly why it is neglected at clinics. The mechanics we must develop under the water do not simulate anything we do in life, so we are teaching a muscle memory that is completely foreign.

The good news is that it is not rocket science. It is 100 percent doable! Any swimmer who chooses to put forth effort on the pull will not only see improvement in swimming times but will also get toned, strong swimmer arms. If that effort is concentrated and nonwavering (in other words, if you keep it slow and easy for the first few weeks and don't bail out on stroke technique in order to keep up with your buddies in the lane), then you are going to see the first signs of improvement within weeks, and continued improvement thereafter as your conditioning and strength kick in.

---

### FOR NEW SWIMMERS

For those of you who are new to swimming, or who have a natural aversion to the water, you will need to spend some time simply getting to know the water and feeling comfortable. Body position is important for you during this time, as is learning how to breathe. Work on keeping your head neutral in the water rather than lifting it (which many new swimmers do when they panic).

The great news is, while you are getting comfortable in the water for a few weeks, you can also train out of the water, developing your pull. This is explained in Chapter 7. The same chapter also explains a number of in-water drills that will be very manageable for you.

# 4

# THEORIES OF PROPULSION
## THE CHALLENGES & THE BEAUTY

**BY NOW YOU ARE SURELY CONVINCED** that the underwater pull should take its place as king of the hill in swimming. I know that once I started laying my bets on it, I made four Olympic teams. There is so much depth and potential in all that is below us when we swim, and I am excited that we are now nearing the part of the book that dives deep into this third dimension.

Before we get into the details that describe the pull and how to develop it, we have a little more foundational work to do; we will draw from it to make the puzzle pieces fit. This final base layer of understanding requires that we revisit the topic of water, this time from a scientific angle—particularly with regard to the study of fluid dynamics. Every textbook on swimming technique includes a significant piece on fluid dynamics as it relates to propulsion, and it is, without fail, the distinguishing topic that gives the book its reputation. Unfortunately, it is also the most laborious, scientific section of the book and for this reason holds the attention of very few readers.

Grasping the concepts of *flow analysis*, *vortex patterns*, and *drag/lift forces* is no small task, so readers have a tendency to gravitate to the sections of the book that are more easily understood (i.e., body position, hip rotation, head position). Because I have opened a can of worms by convincing you that the underwater pull is the most vital aspect of the stroke, I feel obligated to present the theories on swimming propulsion in terms that not only are understandable but also frame the sport on an entirely new level for you.

You are going to learn the origins of much of what you may have heard from fellow athletes, coaches, and even that guy in the lane next to you at the health club who offers his two cents on how you should pull. If you have heard contradicting information, there is good reason; it is because the paradigms on swimming propulsion theory have shifted throughout the years. Often the swimming world would just be getting comfortable with one theory when another one would come along to take its place. This is due to the nature of the medium in which our sport is contested—water. Water complicates things. Cecil Colwin explains it this way in *Swimming Dynamics*:

> *What happens to water when we swim? The answer is we don't actually know. . . . Biomechanists claim to be able to calculate the forces that swimmers develop in the water, but the trouble with these studies is that they depend on the premise of "essentially still water." Water doesn't obediently stand still while forces act upon it. Consequently, some studies may very well be flawed because they are based on the mechanic of solids rather than those of fluid behavior. (Colwin 1999, 72)*

Colwin continues, "Prominent fluid dynamicists, when asked whether the flow reactions to human swimming propulsion could be analyzed by computer simulation, expressed the opinion that the rapidly changing body configurations of human swimmers almost defy complete analysis" (p. 78).

What does this mean for us? It means that we take this understanding that a human being moving through water is a bugger to analyze and put that in our back pocket as we read about the four main theories of propulsion that have prevailed, at one time or another, during the past 50 years or so. Following is a short synopsis of each.

# THEORIES OF PROPULSION

## NEWTON'S THIRD LAW, BEFORE 1960

The first explanation of what was taking place under the water centered on Newton's third law: For every action there is an equal and opposite reaction. Prior to the 1960s, swimming theorists believed that the arm and hand acted as a "paddle" that pushed straight back, with the equal and opposite reaction being that the swimmer moved forward.

Any deviation from a straight path back was a fault in stroke technique because it veered the swimmer away from the fullest application of Newton's third law. Stroking this way meant that a swimmer was operating solely on the fore-aft dimension of our three-dimensional sport.

Simple enough. It makes perfect sense.

There was only one problem—the best swimmers in the world were not doing it.

## THE S PULL AND BERNOULLI'S PRINCIPLE, 1960–2000

In the 1960s James "Doc" Counsilman (coach of Mark Spitz at Indiana University and the man credited as perhaps the most pioneering mind in swimming history) captured thousands of photos of Olympic swimmers and noted that not one of them pulled straight back, but rather all were employing an elliptical curved pattern to their stroke.

Counsilman theorized that this elliptical-shaped pull actually made more sense than a straight back pull because Newton's third law didn't apply to fluids in the same manner it did for solids. Once the swimmer's hand/arm (the "paddle") began to apply force, he noted, the water moved, and once the water was set in motion it offered less resistance to the swimmer. Doc concluded that Newton's third law was effective for pushing water back in short increments but not longer increments such as the full length of the underwater stroke. He believed that by moving the hand/arm to an adjacent plane of water either to the side, above, or below, the swimmer would find slower moving or "still" water and could most effectively apply Newton's third law again.

Counsilman shared his theory with the swim community, and coaches digested it easily since it preserved most of the commonly held action-reaction beliefs of the time. However, Doc had more to share, and it was the second part that caused a stir. He believed that the lateral and vertical stroking patterns seen in the great swimming champions were not just a necessary evil for the swimmer to move to an adjacent plane of still water, but that propulsive force was actually generated by these movements—even more force than back-pressing offered.

Doc pointed out that just as a propeller-driven boat is faster than a paddle-driven boat, so too is a swimmer who operates the hands/arms like a propeller (elliptical pattern) faster than a swimmer who operates the limbs like a paddle (straight back). He backed up this claim with science, introducing lift forces and Bernoulli's principle to the swimming world for the first time in his 1970 article, "The Application of Bernoulli's Principle to Human Propulsion in Water."

Counsilman's Bernoulli theory became known as the "S pull," and it swung the pendulum. Newton's third law and back pressing motions took a back seat and the S pull/Bernoulli theory took the spotlight.

The 1970s were a decade of great change. Swimmers around the world began to not just incorporate but *emphasize* propeller-like movements on the lateral and vertical dimensions alongside their back-pressing strokes.

## CECIL COLWIN AND VORTICES, SINCE THE 1990S

Cecil Colwin was Doc's peer on the other side of the world. His swimmers in South Africa were breaking world records and winning Olympic medals. Colwin was a prolific writer, and in his book *Swimming into the 21st Century*, he acknowledged Doc's discovery: "Counsilman's study showed that, in all the swimming strokes, the pull does not follow a straight line but is composed of short sculling motions, or impulses, that change direction as the hand moves in a curved path across the line of a swimmer's forward movement" (Colwin 1992, 20).

However, while Colwin agreed that the hand indeed navigated a curvilinear path, he was skeptical about whether swimmers could generate propulsion in the same manner propellers do. To Colwin, a swimmer's propulsion was much more akin to nature's flight than engineered flight; hence he studied the wing actions of birds and insects. He noted that as the wings of a bird or insect oscillate, air begins to circulate around the wing, and this creates a *vortex*—fluid that rotates around an axis. It is the vortex circulation that generates propulsion. Similarly, Colwin claimed, the lateral and elliptical stroking movements of a swimmer's hands/arms starts fluid circulation that "wraps" around the limb, forming a vortex that generates propulsion.

Colwin ultimately pioneered a worthy explanation of swimming propulsion when he connected vortex science with the swim stroke. In his book *Swimming Dynamics*, he writes:

> *A vortex is a mass of fluid that rotates about an axis. . . . A vortex is a form of kinetic energy, the energy of motion. A shed vortex represents the energy produced by a swimmer and "given" to the water. When you see vortices produced by the swimmer in water, you are actually looking at the swimmer's propulsion. . . . Vortices often become visible to the underwater viewer when a swimmer is moving at top speed and accidentally entraps air into the stroke. (Colwin 1999, 74)*

Colwin coached his swimmers to become "shapers of the flow," explaining that every time the hand makes a directional change to an adjacent plane of water, the existing vortex that was bound around the limb is shed, and a new one quickly formed. Colwin also believed that vortices form around the feet during the kicking action and are shed at the finish of each kick.

In sum, while Colwin agreed with Counsilman about the curved path of the stroke, he encouraged swimmers to be sensitive to flow circulations and not become "mechanical" in their stroking actions.

## NEWTON'S THIRD LAW WITH DIAGONAL COMPONENTS, SINCE 2000

The most recent theory comes from Ernie Maglischo, renowned writer and swim coach whose teams captured 13 NCAA Division II titles.

In the 1980s Maglischo believed, in agreement with Doc Counsilman, that the hands/arms of elite swimmers appeared to move more on the lateral and vertical dimensions than the fore-aft dimension, and therefore Bernoulli's theory was the only logical explanation for human swimming propulsion. He published his first book, *Swimming Faster*, in 1982, focusing on Bernoulli's principle and the exact hand angles that simulate propeller-blade movements and maximize propulsion.

As research continued in the 1990s, however, two findings cast a shadow over Bernoulli's principle and the S pull. First, it was brought to light that Bernoulli's principle was not applicable to human swimming propulsion, because a swimmer's hand/arm is neither contoured properly nor smooth enough to sustain a boundary layer over its surface (a boundary layer is a thin layer of fluid that is in contact with the surface of the object over which fluid flows, and it is a requisite for Bernoulli's principle). At the same time, new research and computer simulations showed that pressing straight back on the water yielded more force than lateral and vertical propeller-blade stroking motions.

Ernie went back to the drawing board and looked closely at the S pull. How valid was it if Bernoulli's principle could no longer explain it and if back-pressing motions appeared more effective than a lateral sweep? Should swimmers focus on pushing straight back, as was taught during the 1960s?

Like Doc, he found that swimmers could apply propulsive force more effectively if they navigated away from moving water and onto an adjacent plane of still water. He also cited that a curved path back is longer than a straight path back, and longer is better, because swimmers can apply propulsive force over more distance and for a longer period of time on each stroke. Although the amount of force generated by the hand/arm positioned at an angle is slightly less than if the hand/arm faces directly back and pushes 100 percent against the water, the difference is negligible and more than made up for by the longer stroking path. He also concluded that stroking directly back requires athletes to maintain high rates of turnover to keep up with the moving water, which is an inefficient use of the swimmer's energy.

Maglischo determined that the curved path was warranted, but he encouraged swimmers to focus the majority of their efforts on pushing back, and to move laterally only to the extent that it directs the hand/arm to an adjacent plane of water where back-pressing can be more effectively applied and the stroke path is lengthened. He retracted his 1980s claims that encouraged emphasis on lateral movements and rewrote his texts to encourage an emphasis on back-pressing stroking motions.

He makes clear, however, that an emphasis on back-pressing motions does not mean swimmers should return to the straight-back path of the 1960s. The curved path is important. He writes, "Swimmers do not push the arms straight back through the water, rather, they seem to push back against the water as they stroke diagonally through it" (Maglischo 2003, 33).

## THE S-PULL DEBATE

Significant debate is swirling around this topic on pool decks worldwide. That's great, because varying opinions are healthy for progress in any endeavor. But one particular point relating to swim propulsion theory is stifling the progress of many swimmers. That malefactor is the S pull.

Since the early 2000s there has been a concerted effort by many coaches and federations such as USA Swimming to eliminate the S pull from teaching and semantics due to the fact that science has raised questions over such a path.

However, in an effort to address the concerns, we've created a problem by swinging the pendulum too far in the opposite direction. Now, many coaches instruct swimmers to pull straight back.

Highly conscientious swimmers are suffering the most. They are taking the "straight back" cues literally, only to find that this instruction not only slows their speed but in many cases has even caused shoulder injuries.

To illustrate the difference between a curved pull path ("S-shaped," if you choose) versus one that is purely straight back, frames 1–3 in Figure 4.1 show

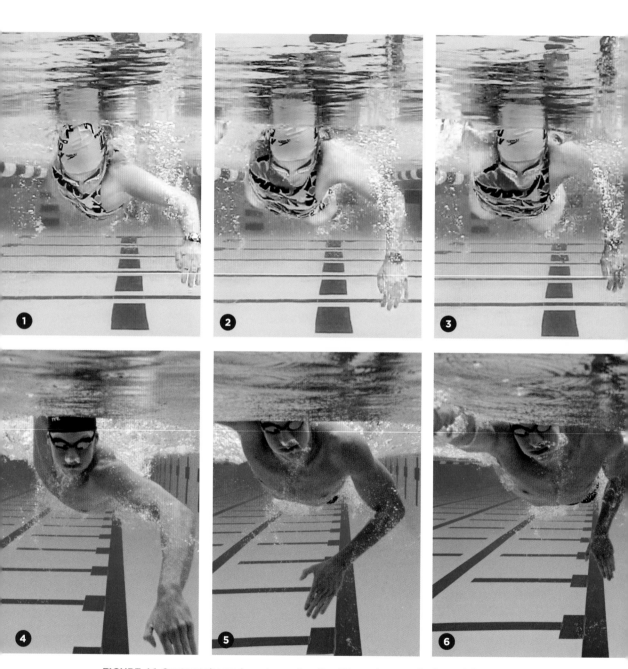

**FIGURE 4.1** Contrast the underwater pull path of the swimmer who is applying the straight-back path in frames 1–3 with that of America's fastest 200 freestyler, Townley Haas, in frames 4–6.

a swimmer who has diligently practiced eliminating any curve or S from her stroke in an effort to achieve a straight-back path.

Contrast frames 1–3 with frames 4–6, which show the stroke path of America's fastest 200 freestyler, Townley Haas.

The difference in the direction and shape of the two paths is significant. We can clearly see that Haas does not pull straight back but rather employs a curve to his propulsive stroking path.

Since the 1960s, coaches and researchers have agreed that elite swimmers push back on the water and incorporate a curve to their path. The question is, which action is more *prominent* in the stroke? Do elite swimmers emphasize back-pushing movements, or do they emphasize lateral sweeps and curved motions?

Ah, now we arrive at the sticking point! The reason there has been a tendency to subscribe to one or the other is because of the inseparable yet fallible association between the S pull and Bernoulli's principle.

As I noted earlier, the 1970s emphasis on lateral movements was named the S pull, and these lateral movements were associated with Bernoulli's principle. The S pull has been associated with Bernoulli's principle from the start.

So, when Bernoulli's principle was disproven as a credible explanation for human swimming propulsion, the S pull got tossed with it. And "S" has been a four-letter word ever since.

But remember, Doc Counsilman's observation was simply that the fastest swimmers do not pull straight back. They take a curved, elliptical, S-shaped path back. Doc may have been wrong in attributing Bernoulli's principle to what he saw, and likening the motion to propeller blades and encouraging swimmers to exploit lateral movements, but he wasn't wrong in what he saw: the curved path. And if he looked at today's swimmers he would say the same thing—it is a curved path.

It's time to release the S from Bernoulli's principle so we can clear up the confusion plaguing many swimmers. By cutting the ties, we won't feel the need to describe the pull path as straight back for fear that noting any curve may convict us of subscribing to the S pull and Bernoulli's principle.

I am not suggesting that we again call this elite stroking motion the S pull. What we choose to call the stroking motion is just semantics. I believe Ernie Maglischo's description is most fitting: "Swimmers should push predominantly *back* on the water as they stroke *diagonally* through it."

Ernie's description accentuates the back-pressing attributes of the stroke while giving a nod to the slighter (but vital!) curvilinear attributes.

In summary, propulsive stroking mechanics in the freestyle have not changed in decades. The manner in which the swim community tries to describe them has changed, and the scientific attempt at explaining them has changed, but propulsive mechanics have not. The path is curved, and the arm makes very unique movements to achieve this slight yet crucial curve.

# 5

# THE UNDERWATER PULL
## THE VITAL ELEMENT

**WE ARE BUILDING SOMETHING HERE,** and the foundation has just been laid. No matter your goals in swimming, you should have a firm grasp of the big picture. Understanding the theories of propulsion and the rate/stroke equation provides a solid base upon which to build your swim stroke.

We are now ready to look at the vital element in our sport—the underwater pull. The pull doesn't earn the number one position solely because propulsion and the stroke/rate equation depend on it. It also gets the prize because it is the most complex part of the stroke.

To appreciate that complexity, consider the palette we have at our disposal while pulling: First, the water below us is three-dimensional, with fore-aft, lateral, and vertical components. Second, the pull comes from the arm, which has a wrist, elbow, and shoulder joint. At any given moment during the propulsive stroking motion, each of those joints is doing something on each of those dimensions. It's an artist's delight down there in the deep blue.

The variety of swim strokes I see at my clinics never ceases to bring happiness to my heart, but the fact remains that science, physics, and mechanics are not so tolerant. They demand more measured actions when it comes to performance. In this chapter we will hone in on the specific stroking actions of elite swimmers and study the path that maximizes propulsion. Olympic medalists have navigated this path for decades, and so can you.

If this sounds like I'm boxing you into an unforgiving, robotic stroke that leaves no room for personal style, rest assured, there is room for freedom in your stroking motion. The path is neither 100 percent literal nor exact. It is better described as having parameters.

For purposes of visualizing those parameters, elite stroking mechanics can be likened to a hurricane cone on a weather channel. When a hurricane barrels up the Gulf of Mexico, for example, forecasters show the path it could take, cautioning that it may hit anywhere from Pensacola to New Orleans.

Swimming mechanics are the same. No swimmer strokes exactly like another, but all elite swimmers make mechanical movements within a range on each of the three dimensions at various phases of their stroke. The best swimmers never stray outside that range. Why? Because going outside the parameters will either limit the effectiveness of propulsion/speed or place the swimmer in a weakened or precarious position, risking injury.

Let's look at the "hurricane cone" of the pull.

## THE PULL PATH

The propulsive path, which I refer to as "the pull," can be broken into three phases: the catch, the diagonal, and the finish. Together, these phases move a swimmer forward in the water. (The nonpropulsive phases of the arm stroke—overwater recovery, entry, and extension—will be discussed in Chapter 6.)

This chapter will make it clear that the path elite swimmers navigate during these phases is curved, not straight back. That curve is slight, and so it may seem insignificant compared to the back-pressing aspects. But although the lateral and vertical movements are not dominant, they are decidedly there, and they are vital.

Let's start with the first phase, the catch.

## THE CATCH

The catch phase of the stroke is when propulsion begins. It commences after the hand/arm enters the water and extends forward. The catch is the only propulsive phase of the stroke that takes place overhead. Many swimmers don't think of this phase as overhead because the arm appears simply to be in front of the body/head. Keep in mind, though, that the body is oriented horizontally in the water, and if we were to orient it vertically, the arm/hand would be overhead. This overhead position is primarily what makes the catch so challenging.

The goal of the catch is to transition the limb from the down-facing position we see during extension to a back-facing position, so propulsion can begin.

Figure 5.1 shows Townley extending in frame 1 and making the catch in frame 2. Note how his arm remains overhead as the forearm and hand transitions from down-facing extension in frame 1 to the back-facing catch in frame 2.

**FIGURE 5.1** To make an elite catch, Townley Haas transitions from a down-facing arm position during extension (1) to a back-facing position (2) while his arm remains overhead.

To illustrate further, head-on photos of the catch in Figure 5.2 span the decades, revealing how this critical element consistently shows up in the strokes of top swimmers.

A swimmer must attend to four details to achieve the back-facing overhead catch position we see in Figures 5.1 and 5.2:

- Press the scapula forward.
- Medially rotate the upper arm.
- Bend the elbow to achieve proper hand depth.
- Sweep the upper arm outside of shoulder width.

Let's examine each detail:

### Press the Scapula Forward

Overhead activity requires that an athlete become familiar with the scapula (shoulder blade) and the muscles that attach to it. In Figure 5.1, we see the engagement of the muscles that surround Townley's scapula both during extension and the catch.

To feel this motion, raise your hand above your head so your shoulder brushes against your face. Notice how you must use the muscles in your back to press your scapula up in such a way that your shoulder touches your chin/cheek area (or your ear if you have very good scapular mobility). This is extension in your swim stroke, and it comes from the scapula.

The scapular engagement that starts during extension must be maintained throughout the catch phase so that the hand/arm stays overhead.

In Figures 5.1 and 5.2, the shoulder juts up against the cheek/chin/ear in every photo—a telltale sign that these swimmers are engaging the muscles around the scapula.

### Medially Rotate the Upper Arm

Medial rotation is a twisting of the upper arm in order to direct the elbow slightly *up*. This feature is why some swimmers and coaches refer to the catch as a "high elbow" catch.

**FIGURE 5.2** The catch has been a feature in the strokes of Olympic champions for decades: Mike Troy in 1960 (1), Mark Spitz in 1972 (2), Ashley Whitney in 1996 (3), and Townley Haas in 2016 (4).

  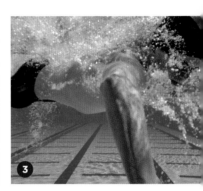

**FIGURE 5.3** Townley medially rotates his upper arm for the catch. Note the position of the bony tip of the elbow as the series progresses.

Don't let the term fool you. Many athletes think "high-elbow" means they must hold the elbow as high in the water as possible. But "high elbow" does not refer as much to the height of the elbow in the water as it does the upward-directing orientation of the joint.

Referring back to Figure 5.1, note that the bony tip of Townley's elbow points to the side of the pool in frame 1 during extension (no medial rotation), and then directs up in frame 2 during the catch (medial rotation).

Figure 5.3 offers a close-up view of Townley medially rotating his upper arm as he transitions from the extension phase (frame 1) to the catch (frames 2 and 3). In frame 1, the bony tip of his elbow points to the side, while in frames 2 and 3 the elbow directs slightly up. This is medial rotation.

While this movement is slight, with the arm rotating just a few degrees, I promise this barely noticeable feature is the difference between championship mechanics and "maybe I should just head to the hot tub" mechanics. You must attend to medial rotation if you hope to get faster, because the action turns on your powerful lat muscles.

Rotate just to where you feel the lat muscles engage (approximately 2–3 centimeters). Take care not to overrotate the upper arm, as impingement of the shoulder tendons/ligaments could occur. Monitor the sensations in your rotator cuff area. If there is any sign of impingement or painful strain, then you have gone too far with the motion.

While medially rotating, most swimmers do not hold the elbow at the surface when they catch. Rather, they angle the upper arm slightly down in the water so the elbow sits below the surface. Exactly how deep it sits during the catch varies, but the range is 3–10 inches. In frame 2 of Figure 5.1, Townley's elbow sits just a few inches below the surface. However, Olympic gold medalist Jack Conger approaches the outer range of our hurricane cone parameters when it comes to elbow depth at the catch. Figure 5.4 shows his preference to position the arm deeper. But note that he medially rotates his upper arm. It is a medially rotated upper arm that defines championship "high elbow" catch mechanics, not elbow depth.

Find the depth that is ideal for you by testing your arm at different depths. If you feel too rigid holding your elbow near the surface, then lower it to a depth where you can function athletically without rigidity.

### Bend the Elbow to Achieve Proper Hand Depth

We're not finished with your elbow yet.

Look again at Figures 5.1 and 5.4 and note the difference between frames 1 and 2. During extension, both Townley's and Jack's arms are straight (frame 1),

**FIGURE 5.4** Although Jack positions his elbow deep at the catch (2) after extending (1), he medially rotates his upper arm to orient the elbow "up"—the key to the "high elbow."

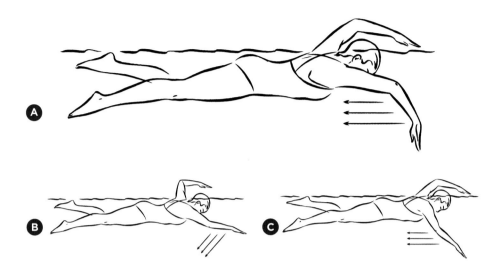

**FIGURE 5.5** Bending the elbow while the arm is overhead (A) is key for a backward press that moves a swimmer forward. A straight arm places force downward (B), delaying the backward press (C).

but their elbows are bent for the catch (frame 2). Elite swimmers gradually bend the elbow as they navigate the catch in order to face the hand/forearm back on the water.

Elbow bend ultimately dictates hand depth. During extension, the hand is just below the surface, but at the catch, the hand is approximately 2 feet deep.

Hand depth is a key feature in an elite catch, but it is important to note that Olympic swimmers achieve this depth not by pressing the hand down with a straight arm, but rather by bending the elbow.

Bending the elbow while the arm is overhead is challenging, so many swimmers make the mistake of pressing the arm straight down in the water, as depicted in Figure 5.5B. These swimmers eventually achieve hand depth and a back-facing position of the hand/arm, as shown in Figure 5.5C, but it is delayed and much less "overhead" (as compared with a proper catch, shown in Figure 5.5A). Worse, shoulder injury often accompanies such a method.

To avoid the mistake of pressing the arm down in the water, focus on continuing to direct the *upper arm* forward even while bending at the elbow to achieve hand depth. This forward-directing upper arm is *not* gliding, however. Gliding implies passivity, as though the entire arm simply stays in a horizontal extended position, with the hand near the surface for a free ride. That is not what is happening. Rather, there is a great deal of athleticism taking place to position the hand deeper in the water.

Figure 5.6 defines these specific catch mechanics with STGRID measurements. The grid helps us see the difference between gliding and elite technique. If Townley were to glide, then he would hold the position we see in frame 1. But we see instead that it is only his upper arm that continues forward. He bends his elbow and directs his hand/forearm down for the catch. Count the grid lines and note how his elbow advances forward, as his hand gets deeper, in every frame. The critical message here is that he does not pull his *upper arm* back as he bends the elbow to make the catch.

Johnny Weissmuller describes the catch, including this forward-directing mentality, beautifully in his book *Swimming the American Crawl*: "The upper arm should be raised, the elbow pointing upward to permit the forearm to hang down almost perpendicularly, and then go forward on a sort of pendulum swing" (Weissmuller 1930, 15).

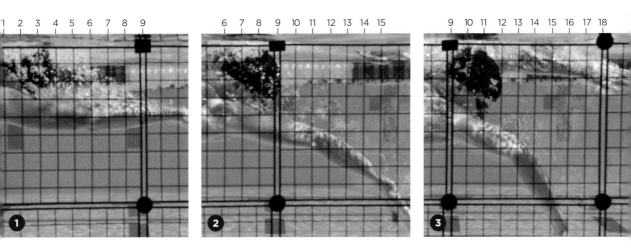

**FIGURE 5.6** Grid lines reveal how Townley's upper arm/elbow advances forward as his hand gets deeper in every frame. This is a championship catch.

It is easy to see why Weissmuller was able to post a 57.4 in the 1920s with a head/body position far less streamlined than any swimmer today. He didn't let two of the most critical stroking details slip past his attention. He describes medial rotation with the words "the elbow pointing upward," and even more sophisticated is his phrase "permit the forearm to hang down *almost perpendicularly*, and then *go forward* on a sort of pendulum swing." Can you see this description in the grid photos of Townley's stroke? Townley bends his elbow so the forearm hangs almost perpendicularly, yet the limb has a forward pendulum look to it because he does not pull the upper arm back.

### Sweep the Upper Arm Outside of Shoulder Width

Elite swimmers have what I call "width to the catch," meaning that the elbow and hand make the catch at a position that is wider than shoulder width. That width must be navigated. When the arm is extended forward before making the catch, it does so directly in front of the shoulder (explained in Chapter 6), but no elite swimmer makes the catch in front of the shoulder. Rather, the elbow—and by association, the forearm and hand—ultimately positions 4–8 inches (1–2 hand widths) wider than the shoulder.

To achieve width to your catch, sweep the upper arm slightly outward as you medially rotate. The elbow bends during these actions; therefore, a swimmer navigates both width and depth for the catch simultaneously.

Figure 5.7 shows Olympic gold medalist Peter Vanderkaay navigating the catch alongside Townley navigating the catch. In frames 1 and 5, both swimmers extend the arm in front of the shoulder, with the hand and forearm just below the surface. Each subsequent frame shows the hand getting deeper due to gradual elbow bend, and the arm sweeping wide of shoulder width (and medially rotating). Of course, it's all happening overhead because the upper arm directs forward, rather than pulling back, throughout the process.

Note one nuance between Peter and Townley: Peter primarily feels for depth before navigating width, and Townley primarily feels for width before getting depth. Either is fine, because both end up at the same place in frames 4 and 8—a championship catch!

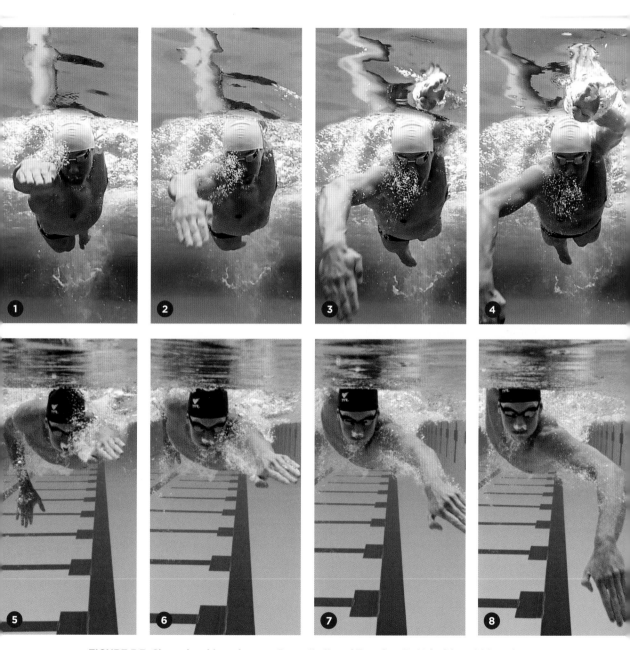

**FIGURE 5.7** Championship swimmers Peter (1–4) and Townley (5–8) feel for width and depth as they make the catch.

Figure 5.7 shows that Townley gets slightly more width to his catch than Peter, but both are within those hurricane cone parameters (4–8 inches, or 1–2 hand widths wider than the shoulder).

To determine your own perfect catch width, play around within the range of 4–8 inches, or 1–2 hand widths, wider than shoulder width, and wherever you feel the tendons and ligaments line up without strain, you've found your width. Notice how even 1–2 inches difference—either narrower or wider—from your ideal position feels like the tendons/ligaments are out of alignment. You do not want to feel that, and you shouldn't if you dial in your width.

### Summary for the Catch

The catch phase entails focused movement on just about every dimension *other than back-pressing.* The upper arm presses *forward* and rotates *up*, while the hand finds *depth*, and the entire limb gets *width*. These actions result in an arm that is in a strong position, facing back on the water. Believe in this. The unique work you did to make the catch pays off in the upcoming phases of the pull.

## THE DIAGONAL

After the catch, we enter the diagonal, or middle phase, of the pull. This phase is often referred to as the power phase. The word "power" gives us our first clue that the theories of propulsion are at play.

I call this middle phase "the diagonal" partly because I find Ernie Maglischo's description of the stroking motion most fitting: push predominantly back on the water while stroking *diagonally* through it. This phase is when we see the first diagonal direction to the back-pressing path.

The word "diagonal" is also appropriate because, when done correctly, the upper arm changes articulation and positions at an angle approximately 45 degrees in relation to the surface of the water.

Figure 5.8 shows elite freestylers during the diagonal phase. Note the 45-degree position of the upper arm in relation to the surface. Notice also that the hand is now under the body. This is our first evidence that elite swimmers

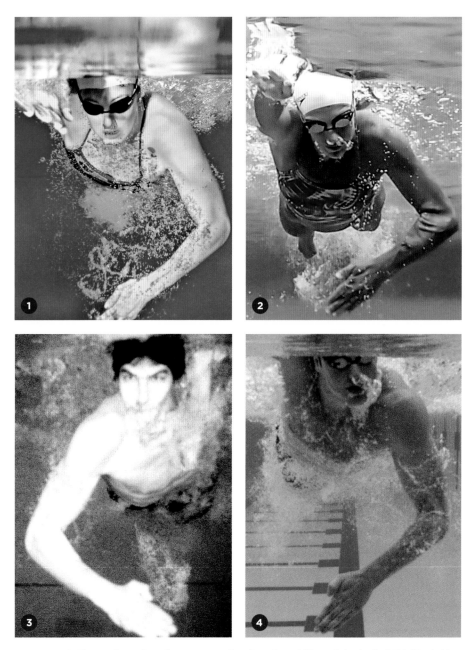

**FIGURE 5.8** These champions from across the decades—Allison Schmitt in 2012 (1), Ashley Whitney in 1996 (2), Mark Spitz in 1972 (3), and Jack Conger in 2016 (4)—are dialing in the diagonal. Note that the hand is under the body.

stroke diagonally back, not straight back. If they were to stroke straight back, we would see the hand wide of shoulder width at this point, as we see at the catch.

To get to an elite diagonal position, you must do the following actions simultaneously:

- Un-rotate the upper arm.
- Deepen the upper arm as you sweep the water back.
- Line up the forearm and hand with the upper arm.

Let's look at these three actions separately.

### Un-rotate the Upper Arm as You Sweep the Water Back

Elite swimmers position the hand under the body during the diagonal. Making your way to this position from the wide-of-shoulder catch position is almost a function of upper arm mechanics, not lower arm mechanics. While it may seem logical to increase elbow bend in order to bring your hand under your body, that is not what elite swimmers do.

Notice in Figure 5.9 that the degree of elbow bend in Townley's stroke is the same in frame 2 (the diagonal) as it is in frame 1 (the catch). Townley achieves the diagonal position not by increasing elbow bend and slicing inward but rather by "un-rotating" his upper arm as he sweeps it back.

Because the catch involves medial rotation of the upper arm, the idea of undoing that motion makes sense. "Un-rotating" brings the upper arm back to a neutral position for this powerful mid-phase of the pull. And the un-rotation action is also what directs the hand diagonally back through the water so that it sweeps under the body. Some elite swimmers sweep the hand just under the hip, while others sweep under the belly button. You are within elite parameters if your hand ends up somewhere under your body between your hip and belly button.

Note the difference in the orientation of the elbow joint in Figure 5.9. The elbow points up in frame 1 (the catch) and to the side in frame 2 (the diagonal). This reflects the "un-rotation" movement from catch to diagonal. Note

**FIGURE 5.9** Transitioning from the catch (1) to the diagonal (2) is a function of upper-arm mechanics.

how this action also changes the position of the hand in the water. In frame 1, Townley's fingers point to the bottom of the pool, and in frame 2 the hand angles diagonally.

Figure 5.10 is a close-up view of this un-rotation action. Townley's elbow directs up (medial rotation) during the catch in frame 1, and then to the side of the pool during the diagonal phase in frame 2. Un-rotation comes from the upper arm.

Finally, notice in Figure 5.10 how Townley's arm sweeps back in the water between frame 1 (the catch) and frame 2 (the diagonal). This is the moment in the stroke when the work you did to position the arm facing back on the water during the catch pays off. You now have a mass of water you can powerfully sweep back, and sweep back you should!

**FIGURE 5.10** Note the change in elbow position as Townley un-rotates his upper arm while transitioning from the catch (1) to the diagonal (2).

### Deepen the Upper Arm as You Sweep the Water Back

While un-rotating and sweeping the arm back, the elbow deepens slightly on the vertical dimension. Elite swimmers do not pull horizontally back after making the catch. Rather, the upper arm changes its articulation in the water. Figure 5.11 shows the degree to which Townley's upper arm/elbow deepens from the catch to the diagonal. Note the 1½ grid-line difference in the height of his elbow between frame 1 (the catch) and frame 2 (the diagonal).

As with many stroking details, this difference in elbow height is slight but critical, both in terms of propulsion and shoulder health.

### Line Up the Forearm and Hand with the Upper Arm

The upper arm is the star of the show during the diagonal phase, but the details of the lower arm need mention, too. In all the photos thus far, notice how the hand and forearm keep pace with the action of the upper arm. The hand/forearm lines up with the upper arm to act as one paddle.

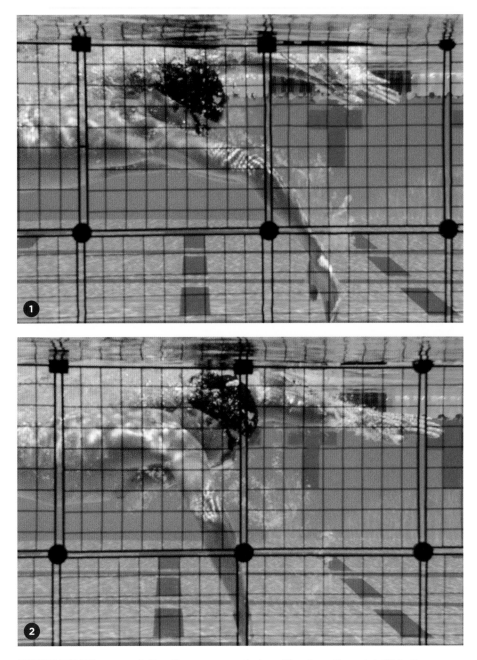

**FIGURE 5.11** When un-rotating the upper arm to transition from the catch (1) to the diagonal (2), elbow height lowers on the vertical dimension.

Figure 5.12 shows Jack in the diagonal phase. Notice how every part of the arm lines up on the fore-aft dimension. The diagonal is a very powerful phase if a swimmer creates a giant paddle like we see in Jack's stroke, because a large mass of water is accelerated back.

A common error during the diagonal phase is to "drop" the elbow on the fore-aft dimension, causing the hand to trail behind the upper arm, rather than lining up with it. The result is a loss of propulsion as the forearm/hand slip somewhat horizontally through the water. This is depicted in Figure 5.13. Notice in this photo how the hand and forearm are not lined up with the upper arm on the fore-aft dimension as they are in Figure 5.12. ("Dropping" the elbow on the fore-aft dimension is to be distinguished from lowering the arm on the vertical dimension as just described.)

**FIGURE 5.12** Jack lines up his upper arm, forearm, and hand to act as a giant paddle on the fore-aft dimension during the diagonal phase of the stroke.

**FIGURE 5.13** A dropped elbow during the diagonal phase causes the hand to trail behind the upper arm on the fore-aft dimension, resulting in a loss of propulsion and speed.

## Oarlocks

You can do everything correctly during the diagonal yet lose propulsion if one detail is not on your radar. I call this detail *oarlocks*.

Over the years, I'd noted at my clinics that some swimmers appeared to apply solid mechanics yet did not move forward as fast as they should based on their fitness and technique. This was perplexing. Upon close review of underwater film, I noticed that these swimmers were pulling their shoulder back during the diagonal phase of the stroke (specifically, sliding their scapula back, which in turn moved the shoulder back). A gap formed between the shoulder and the cheek/chin.

Elite freestylers do not do this. Rather, they maintain scapular stability—or a shoulder shrug—as they navigate the diagonal phase of the stroke, leaving no gap between the shoulder and chin.

> ## OSCILLATING
>
> I describe the propulsive stroking actions during the catch and diagonal as a "rotation" and "un-rotation" of the upper arm, but Cecil Colwin uses the word "oscillate" to describe the same action. I find tremendous value in his description. The wings of a bird or insect oscillate to generate propulsion, and this is very much akin to the rotation/un-rotation action of a swimmer's upper arm. Use Colwin's cue if it helps you to understand the unique upper arm rotational attributes of elite stroking.

I call what I observed the oarlocks shrug, and it involves the effective transfer of power. In rowing, oarlocks on a boat act like a fulcrum so the propulsive force a rower exerts on the water with the oar(s) transfers to moving the boat forward. Oars pivot around the pin of an oarlock, but the oarlock is bolted down. It does not slide back and forth, nor does it move up and down. If an oarlock on the boat is not bolted down, then power dissipates out of the unstable oarlock rather than transferring to thrust the boat forward.

Consider this concept in cycling. A cyclist does not want the hips to move up and down when pedaling; if a cyclist rocks the hips in the saddle, then power that should go into the pedal stroke instead dissipates out through the unstable hip. The hip is the oarlock and must remain still.

The same is true for swimming. A swimmer exerts force on the water with the limbs, and this force must be transferred in order to move the body forward. The shoulder is the swimmer's oarlock, connecting the arm to the body. While the upper arm rotates for the catch and then un-rotates for the diagonal, the shoulder itself should remain stable. If the shoulder slides back during moments of the stroke that call for transfer of power, then some amount of propulsive thrust will dissipate out of the unstable shoulder rather than moving the swimmer forward.

In order to ensure stable oarlocks during the propulsive arm stroking motion, make sure that you maintain a shrug in your shoulder during the diagonal phase of the stroke. The key to this is maintaining scapular stability.

Do not pull the scapula back. The upper arm pivots and sweeps inside the joint as the scapula—and hence the shoulder—remains forward and stable.

Figure 5.14 shows the difference between stable and unstable oarlocks. In frame 1, Jack maintains stable oarlocks. There is no gap between his shoulder and chin. The swimmer in frame 2, however, has not maintained the shoulder shrug. Notice the gap between her shoulder and chin. She is pulling the scapula back, which in turn pulls the shoulder back, resulting in a loss of transfer of power during this incredibly propulsive phase of the stroke.

### Summary for the Diagonal

Propulsion is the name of the game when it comes to the diagonal phase of the stroke. Hold a mass of water on your limb and sweep it back. Do not slip the limb through the water. And always maintain strong, stable oarlocks so the propulsive power from the limb transfers to moving the body forward.

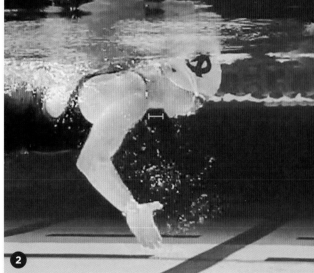

**FIGURE 5.14** Jack strokes with stable oarlocks during the diagonal (1), with no gap between his shoulder and chin. The swimmer in frame 2 strokes with unstable oarlocks; note the gap between her shoulder and chin, resulting in a loss of propulsive power.

## THE FINISH

The catch is a beast, and the diagonal, although easier, is no cakewalk, but the finish is where you get your reward. You travel faster at this moment in the stroke cycle than any other by tending to a few simple details:

- Lift the upper arm from the water as you keep the elbow bent.
- Direct the hand back toward the hip.
- Open up the hip, shoulder, and chest.

Let's examine each of these more closely. All are meant to lengthen this final phase of the propulsive stroking motion.

### Lift the Upper Arm from the Water as You Keep the Elbow Bent

Figure 5.15 shows Jack finishing the stroke. Notice how he lifts his upper arm from the water while keeping his elbow bent. You might think the arm should be straightened at the finish in order to lengthen the stroke. But by keeping the elbow bent and lifting the upper arm from the water, the stroking path extends diagonally back and up (frame 1), which allows for a longer propulsive path than a straight back push with the hand.

Let's look at this bent-elbow aspect of the finish from an above-water view. Figure 5.16 shows Townley lifting his arm from the water while his elbow remains bent.

Good news! At my clinics, where I use video to analyze swimmers' strokes, 95 percent of attendees naturally keep their elbow bent while lifting the upper arm from the water.

### Direct the Hand Back Toward the Hip

While lifting the upper arm from the water, the finish phase entails making the second and final move to an adjacent plane of water. In Figure 5.17 note how Jack's hand changes direction, from under the body during the diagonal phase (frame 1) to alongside the hip at the finish (frame 2). He presses diagonally back through the water. To achieve this, simply change the pitch of the

**FIGURE 5.15** To finish the stroke, Jack keeps his elbow bent as he lifts his upper arm from the water. This lengthens his stroking path diagonally back and up as depicted by the yellow line in frame 1.

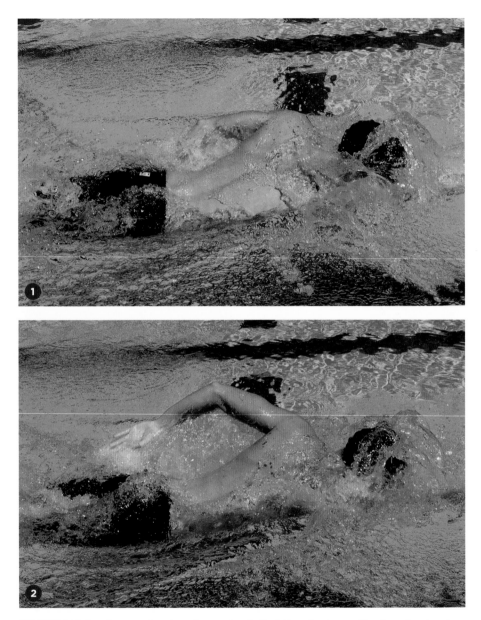

**FIGURE 5.16** An above-water view shows clearly that Townley keeps his elbow bent as he finishes the stroke.

**FIGURE 5.17** Jack's hand changes direction from under the body during the diagonal phase (1) to alongside the hip at the finish (2).

hand to direct the hand toward the hip as you lift the arm from the water. The hand/fingers point toward the bottom of the pool during the finish (frame 2) just as they did during the catch.

More good news! Just as many swimmers naturally keep the elbow bent at the finish, most swimmers naturally pitch the hand toward the hip for the finish.

### Open Up the Hip, Shoulder, and Chest

The final key detail of the finish phase pertains to the hip, chest, and shoulder. Elite swimmers "open up" during the finish to lengthen the stroke. The chest and hip on the finishing side of the body lift (pull open) along with the upper arm that is exiting the water. In addition, the oarlocks shrug from the diagonal

**FIGURE 5.18** Townley lengthens his stroke as he transitions from the diagonal (1) to the finish (2 and 3). Note how his chest opens up and a gap forms between his shoulder and cheek/chin.

phase is no longer held. A gap (the one we did not want during the catch and diagonal) now forms between the shoulder and cheek/chin. The entire torso lengthens.

In Figure 5.18, Townley transitions from the diagonal (frame 1) to the finish (frames 2 and 3). Notice that he lengthens the finishing action by opening the right side of his chest. Also note that the oarlocks shrug seen in frame 1 is no longer held at the finish as he lifts his upper arm from the water.

### Summary for the Finish

The finish is about lengthening the stroke to get the most from this final propulsive thrust. The lengthening actions are intuitive for most athletes on a physical level, but some have a hard time mentally envisioning how a bent arm serves to provide more length. If you're one who is straightening your arm in an attempt to get more from your finish, then make the switch to a bent-arm stroking motion and you'll discover additional forward thrust.

## GRID ANALYSIS FROM EXTENSION TO FINISH

That wraps up the mechanics of the propulsive phases of the stroke. Let's put them together now, with an STGRID placed in front of the swimmer, to get a measured perspective of the movements.

The following series shows Jack from a head-on perspective and Townley from a profile view, navigating from the extension phase of the stroke to the finish. Although we have not yet studied the extension phase (covered in the next chapter), I include it here to reveal the parameters of the catch.

In Figure 5.19 Jack navigates with his left arm from extension in frame 1, to the catch in frame 2, the diagonal in frame 3, and the finish in frame 4. The head-on grid photos of Jack help us understand the curvilinear stroking motions from a lateral and vertical (depth) perspective.

Figure 5.20 shows the fore-aft movements (and vertical/depth again) in Townley's stroke from a profile view.

Note: A = hand; B = elbow; C = shoulder; D = crown of head.

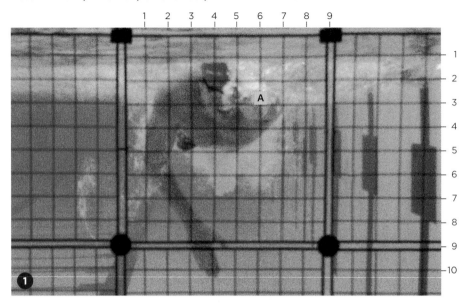

**EXTENSION** Jack's left hand, elbow, and shoulder share the same point on the grid lines (A). He extends in a straight line, directly in front of his shoulder.

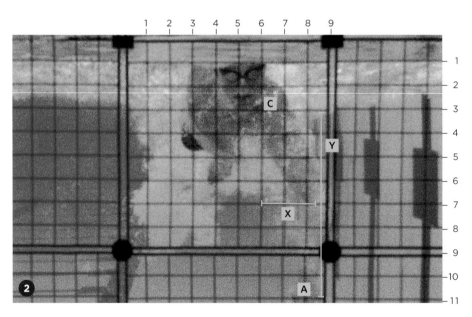

**CATCH** *Width:* The elbow and hand are 2.5 grid lines wider at the catch than they were at extension (the distance marked X).
*Depth:* Jack's hand is a full grid square deeper (the distance marked Y).

**FIGURE 5.19**

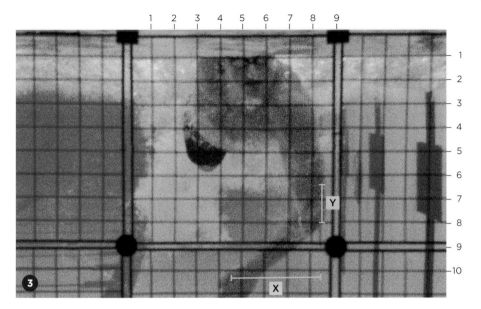

**DIAGONAL** Jack's hand moves in 4 grid lines, from 8.5 during the catch to 4.5 during the diagonal (the distance marked X). His elbow deepens 1.5 grid lines, from 6.5 to 8 on the vertical dimension (the distance marked Y).

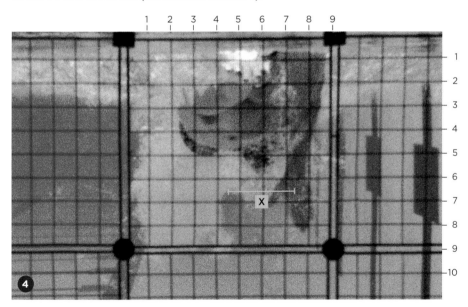

**FINISH** The hand moves out 3 grid lines, from 4.5 at the diagonal to 7.5 to finish next to the hip (the distance marked X). The hand, elbow, and shoulder also lift from their deeper positions at the diagonal.

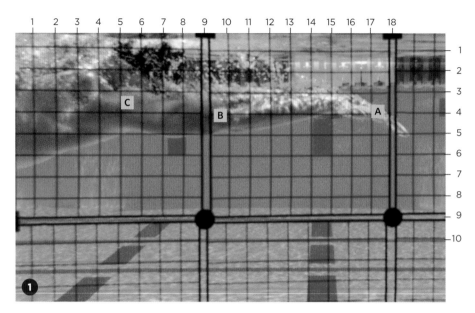

**EXTENSION** Townley's arm, from fingertip to shoulder, extends horizontally between grid lines 3 and 4 on the vertical dimension.

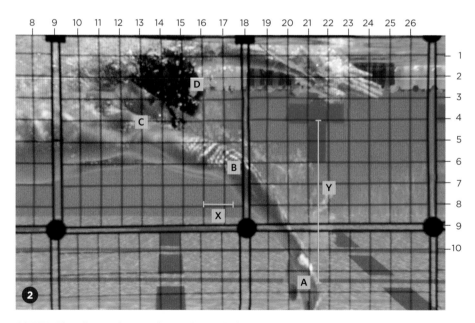

**CATCH** The elbow advances forward 7.5 grid lines from extension to catch (from 10 to 17.5). Also, Townley's elbow is 1.5 grid lines in front of the crown of his head (the distance marked X). His hand moved almost a full grid square deeper (the distance marked Y).

**FIGURE 5.20**

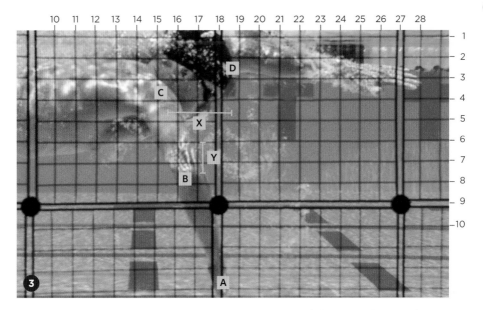

**DIAGONAL** Elbow depth lowers 1.5 grid lines on the vertical dimension from catch to diagonal (the distance marked Y). Also note the stable oarlocks: In frame 2 (the catch) Townley's shoulder is 3 grid lines from the crown of his head (shoulder at 13 and the crown of the head at 16). During the diagonal he maintains the 3 grid-line distance (shoulder at 15.5 and crown of the head at 18.5).

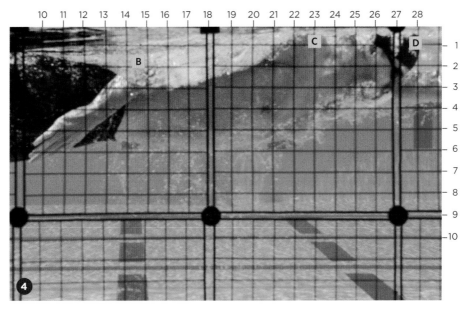

**FINISH** Everything lengthens and lifts. Oarlock shrug no longer held. The distance between Townley's shoulder and crown of head is now 5 grid lines (shoulder at 23 and crown of head at 28).

## DECADES OF COMPARISON

At the start of this chapter I stated that Olympic champions have navigated the same pull parameters for decades. To wrap up our study of the pull path mechanics, let's lay the strokes of gold medalists Mark Spitz (1970s) and Rowdy Gaines (1980s) alongside contemporary swimmers Elizabeth Beisel and Jack Conger as each navigates the catch, diagonal, and finish (Figure 5.21). Notice that all the details explained in this chapter show up in their strokes. The parameters of the freestyle pull path have not changed in decades.

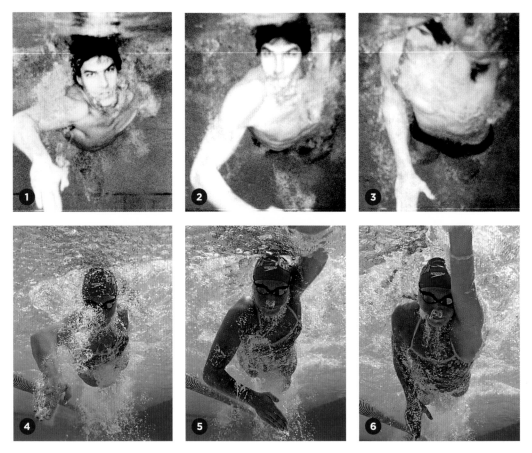

**FIGURE 5.21** Olympic champions throughout the decades have navigated the same propulsive pull path parameters: Spitz (1–3), Beisel (4–6), Gaines (7–9), and Conger (10–12).

## FEEL FOR THE WATER

The parameters of elite mechanics are critical, but their effectiveness can be diminished greatly if a swimmer lacks a "feel" for the water. Some believe a feel for the water is a gift an athlete either has or does not. I disagree wholeheartedly. This vital element of the pull can be taught, and it is accomplished by dialing in *hand speed change* as you navigate the mechanics of the stroke cycle.

The concept of hand speed change must be blended with our study of the theories of propulsion from Chapter 4 to understand what it means to have a

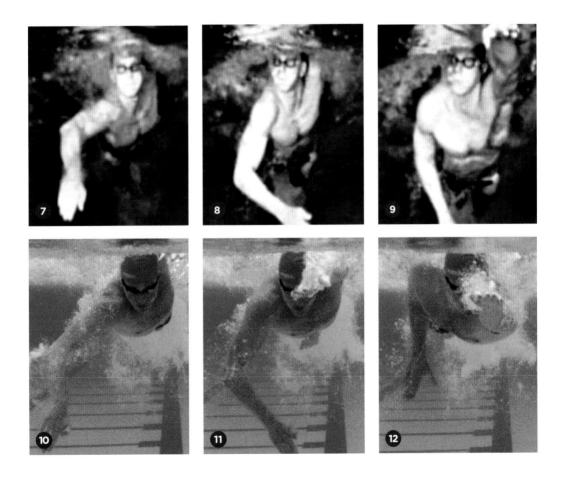

---

### THROWING WATER TAKES FORCE AND ENERGY

Some swimmers misunderstand hand speed change, and they accelerate by dropping the elbow and slipping the hand quickly through the water. They take the path of lesser resistance. Do not do that. Throwing a mass of water takes force/strength. There should be no sensation of "slipping" during the propulsive phases of the stroke.

---

"feel" for the water. Ernie Maglischo explains that swimmers push predominantly back on the water as they stroke diagonally through it. He tips his hat to Newton's third law as a swimmer's source of propulsion.

Newton's third law, however, as it pertains to a fluid is not the same as with a solid. We don't push hard against water thinking it will yield a response. It won't. To get the benefit of Newton's third law in water, swimmers accelerate—or throw—the mass of water that is on their limbs *back*, similar to the manner in which a jet engine on an airplane accelerates air back to generate thrust.

The physics definition of *acceleration* is "the rate of change of velocity per unit of time." Simply stated, it is an "increase of speed." Acceleration does not mean "to go fast." Rather, it means that speed changes, from slower to faster.

Elite swimmers' hands do not move at a constant speed as they progress through the phases of the pull. Hand speed changes, from slowest at the catch to fastest at the finish. In this way they are able to accelerate, or throw, water back.

Controlling hand speed at the catch—so it is "slower"—is achieved by moving the hand/arm on dimensions other than pulling back. To be clear, the hand/arm moves. Do not mistake slow hand speed at the catch as passively gliding in a straight-arm extension position. Rather, it is movement on the lateral and vertical dimensions (getting the width and depth discussed in this chapter) that is the key to "slower" hand speed at the catch. Refrain from rushing to pull back (I call this "yanking" the water).

Once a swimmer makes the catch, he or she has a mass of water on the limb that can be moved back. Gradually build hand speed through the diagonal and finish phases, sensing how you can accelerate the mass back at the end of each phase. An elite swimmer throws water back at the end of the diagonal phase of the stroke and then changes hand direction toward the hip to throw another column of water back at the finish. *Two throws.* Swimmers get more benefit from throwing water back in two shorter increments (one at the diagonal and one at the finish) rather than a single long increment such as a straight back pull from catch to finish.

Avoid abrupt spikes during the diagonal phase because you need to save some for the finish. Acceleration must continue through the finish to have an effective second throw. This is "feel" for the water—thoughtfully building the momentum for two throws.

To master a feel for the water, the key is to be patient at the beginning of the propulsive action so you can build speed for the finish. The back half is where you'll find your reward. The mechanics described in this chapter are critical for establishing arm positions that allow water to be thrown back (rather than to the side, up, or down). Blend them with hand speed change to generate maximal propulsion.

---

### ACCELERATING THE KICK

The same concept of acceleration holds true for the kick. Foot speed must change for water to be thrown off at the finish of the kick. Some swimmers try too hard at the beginning of the kicking action, when the foot is at the surface. If foot speed is too fast at this point, then they are unable to accelerate and throw water off the foot at the finish of the kick. Foot speed may be fast the entire way through, but "fast" is not the same as acceleration. These swimmers lack finesse in their kick and find kicking to be exhausting, with little or no benefit. These swimmers need only focus on changing their foot speed alongside kick mechanics (explained in Chapter 6), and they will become much more fond of this propulsive action.

# 6

# THE OTHER 80 PERCENT

## A REVIEW OF THE NONVITAL ELEMENTS

**I'VE MADE A BOLD CLAIM** that pull mechanics and a feel for the water are the vital elements in our sport. Of the 10 things to work on from a technique standpoint, those two have more impact than anything else in terms of a swimmer reaching his/her full potential.

But what about the other 80 percent of technique elements in the freestyle stroke? What's involved in those, and how much should we focus on them?

First, let's name them. Following is my version of Pareto's 80/20 in swimming:

### The Vital Elements: The 20 Percent That Have 80 Percent Impact

- Pull mechanics
- Feel

### The Nonvital Elements: The 80 Percent That Have 20 Percent Impact

- Overwater recovery
- Entry
- Extension

- Axis line balance
- Stroke timing
- Kicking
- Breathing
- Head and body position

The nonvital elements are labeled as such for one or more of the following reasons:

- They do not have the impact on performance that the pull has.
- They cannot be properly applied with poor pull mechanics. In other words, the pull is a prerequisite.
- They are easier to learn than the pull and thus do not demand as much attention.

Don't get the idea, however, that the nonvital elements can be ignored. They do impact performance and thus require attention. My aim in ranking them as nonvital is to emphasize that you should not forgo a focus on the more challenging vital elements while fixating on other parts of the stroke. These aspects should be understood and addressed in appropriate amounts in training.

Let's examine that other 80 percent more closely.

## THE NONPROPULSIVE PHASES OF THE STROKE

In Chapter 5 we studied the three propulsive phases of the arm movement—the catch, diagonal, and finish. The arm stroke also includes three nonpropulsive phases (phases that do not move a swimmer forward): overwater recovery, entry, and extension. While one arm is in a propulsive phase of the stroke, the other is in one of these nonpropulsive phases.

Our objective during these nonpropulsive phases comes down to one or both of the following:

- Reducing resistance: Because these phases do not move us forward, we want to minimize the resistance they cause.
- Establishing rhythm in the stroke: We aim to sync the nonpropulsive movements with the propulsive phases by correlating hand speed change.

## OVERWATER RECOVERY

The overwater recovery phase, which begins immediately after the arm completes the finish phase of the pull, is simply a continuation of the finishing motion—a lifting of the upper arm from the water. I repeat, the overwater recovery begins with a lifting of the upper arm. Many swimmers rush to bring the hand forward after it exits the water, which torques the tendons in the shoulder, potentially causing injury, and also forces a swimmer to rush the catch on the arm that is in the water.

To properly begin the overwater recovery, continue lifting the upper arm as you did during the finish. Your elbow leads the motion. Lifting the arm to start the recovery establishes a vertically oriented upper arm. Elite swimmers do not swing their arm horizontally over the water. They recover it in a much more vertical fashion. Figure 6.1 shows how the lifting motion at the beginning of the overwater recovery establishes that vertical upper arm. Once the upper arm positions

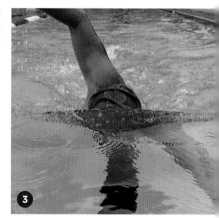

**FIGURE 6.1** Lifting the elbow to start the overwater recovery phase establishes a vertical upper arm position.

in this way, the tendons and ligaments in the shoulder are in a mechanically safe position to recover the hand/arm forward, as shown in frame 3.

To lift your arm in such fashion, draw the scapula toward the midline of the body and tuck your shoulder behind your head. Figure 6.2, frame 1, shows Townley's shoulder tucked behind his head. From a rear-view angle in frame 2, we see the creases in Townley's back, indicating the muscles surrounding the scapula are actively working to pull the scapula in toward the spine. Tipping on your side to position your upper arm vertically does not count. You must use the muscle tissue surrounding your scapula to draw the arm to the correct position.

Along with shoulder health, another important reason for establishing a vertical upper arm recovery is to sync the recovering arm with the arm that is in the water making the catch. Referring back to Figure 6.1, notice that as the recovering arm lifts in frame 2, the catching arm navigates width and depth. *Neither hand/arm moves forward or backward on the fore-aft dimension.* Some swimmers can't resist rushing the hands forward and back during the catch and the beginning of the overwater recovery, but you must have the patience

**FIGURE 6.2** Townley tucks his shoulder behind his head to establish a vertical upper arm recovery (1). He does so by drawing his scapula toward the midline of his body, as shown by the creases in his back (2). Note that he does not rush to bring his hand forward.

to believe in these moments if you are to acquire rhythm and momentum in your stroke.

What about the lower arm? Whereas the upper arm has rules, the lower arm does not. Hold your forearm and hand in any position as your recover over the water. Most textbooks show proper technique as dangling the lower arm so the hand recovers near the surface of the water. This is fine; however, if you look at 10 elite swimmers' overwater recovery technique, you will see half employ this lower arm position while the other half hold the forearm and hand higher.

Figure 6.3 shows Jack and Townley each recovering their arm over the water. Jack holds his forearm and hand higher while Townley recovers his in a dangling textbook fashion. Either position is fine. The common element is a vertically oriented upper arm.

When determining where to hold your lower arm, find a position that is comfortable for you. The most important consideration is that your hand is relaxed, and that the weight of the recovering arm does not strain the shoulder or take "effort" to bring forward.

**FIGURE 6.3** Jack recovers his lower arm high over the water (1) while Townley chooses a more textbook dangled lower arm (2). Either position is fine.

## ENTRY

The vertical upper arm recovery sets you up perfectly to enter your hand in the water in front of your shoulder (or slightly in front of the head), moving in a forward direction.

Athletes who swing the upper arm horizontally over the water during the recovery phase will almost certainly make the mistake of "crossing over" on their entry. Their fingertips may enter in front of the shoulder, as desired, but the direction the hand/arm is traveling at that moment is angled across the line of forward movement, adding unnecessary resistance.

In Figure 6.4, Jack maintains a strong vertical upper arm position even as he nears the final moments of the overwater recovery (frame 1). This sets him up beautifully to enter the water, fingertips in front of his shoulder (frame 2).

## EXTENSION

The extension phase follows immediately after hand entry. Because it takes place in the water and is a nonpropulsive phase, one of our primary tasks is to minimize resistance. To do this, extend the arm forward, directly in front of the shoulder, as shown in Figure 6.5.

**FIGURE 6.4** A proper overwater recovery (1) sets up a swimmer for an ideal entry in front of the shoulder (2).

There is a final nuance to highlight regarding entry and extension. When an elite swimmer's fingertips enter the water, the elbow is held slightly above the water. In Figure 6.6, notice that Townley's elbow is higher than his hand just before entry.

At entry, the hand/arm is angled in such a way that it will pierce downward in the water if it continues its current tracking. However, elite swimmers do not pierce downward on extension. Rather, they extend forward, with the hand and arm just below the surface.

To switch from the angle we see in Figure 6.6 to a streamlined horizontal arm extension, a swimmer must allow

**FIGURE 6.5** Jack extends his arm forward directly in front of his shoulder to minimize resistance during this nonpropulsive phase of the stroke.

the weight of the elbow and upper arm to drop into the water after the fingertips touch the surface. Gravity takes over at this moment. Keep your arm relaxed. Your elbow will "splash" into the water as the arm accelerates forward.

**FIGURE 6.6** Townley's fingertips enter the water before his elbow.

In elite strokes, you will see a splash on both sides of the elbow when it enters the water and shoots forward. Figure 6.7 shows this splash.

Swimmers at my clinics love the splash, but some get so enthusiastic about being permitted to do this that they crash their arm down on the water and forget it is meant to slipstream and accelerate forward. To help you remember to accelerate the extending arm forward, keep in mind that it is synched with the hand that is in the water navigating the back half of the pull.

Look again at Figure 6.7 and note that the hand/arm in the water is nearing the end of the diagonal phase; therefore, that hand/arm is building its acceleration. There is a unique dance that happens between the two arms at this point. The extending arm accelerates forward and immediately cues the finishing arm to accelerate the next moment. It's a 1-2 dance. Extend and accelerate, then finish and accelerate.

Now for the best part: Immediately after these acceleration moments, you reenter the catch on one arm and the overwater recovery on the other, so hand speed slows again. From acceleration to slowing, you create impulse and rhythm to your stroke! You're dancing in the water.

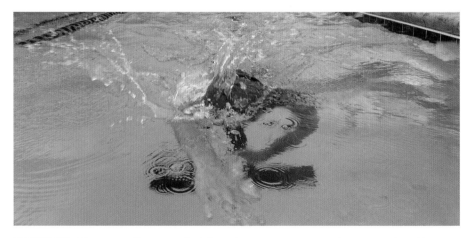

**FIGURE 6.7** Allow your elbow to splash into the water as you accelerate your hand/arm forward on extension.

## AXIS LINE BALANCE

Next let's study the core of the body. Much of what is said about the core is often expressed in one word: rotate. Describing core movement with this single word is vague, leaving too much room for misinterpretation. There are different parts of the core (the torso, shoulders, hips), and each moves uniquely. To clump their movements under the word "rotate" does not do justice to details of the scene.

Let's start with the torso, namely the ribs and chest. Freestyle is a "long axis" stroke. This means a swimmer rides an axis line the length of the torso. Imagine dividing your body in half, a left side and right side, the mid-line passing through the bellybutton. When an elite swimmer extends an arm forward in the water, he/she balances and rides on the axis line on that side of the body.

Where is the line located on the body? The line you want to ride is frontal, located on your chest/stomach, and exactly halfway between your belly button and your side. Many swimmers who hear the word "rotate" think it is best to tip fully onto their side with belly button pointing to the wall of the pool. Elite technique is more refined and balanced than that. It must be, if a swimmer is to seamlessly make the switch from one axis line to the other.

Figure 6.8 shows Peter balanced on the axis line on the left side of his body. He has not tipped onto his side; rather, he is balancing on the line midway between his belly button and side of his body. We could view this as balancing and riding on the front of the ribcage, or, since a male swimmer's suit does not cover the chest, we can also see that the axis line runs through the nipple.

Figure 6.9 shows Townley balancing on the axis line from a profile view. From this vantage point we can see how Townley maintains his balance on the left side of his body as he lifts his

**FIGURE 6.8** Peter balances on the axis line on the left side.

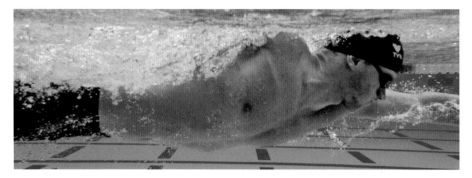

**FIGURE 6.9** Townley balances the axis line on the left frontal side of his body while he lifts his right arm from the water. He does not tip on his side as he lifts his arm.

right arm from the water for the finish and recovery phases. He does not tip on his side but rides a frontal axis line even as the other half of his body is engaged in the actions of the other phases of the stroke.

Knowing when to switch to the axis line on the other side of the body is important for maintaining a fluid stroke. Elite swimmers ride the axis line on one side of their body during the extension, catch, and diagonal phases of the stroke. While beginning the finish, the arm on the other side is in the extension phase, and it is during this time the swimmer seamlessly switches to the axis line on that side of the body.

Figure 6.10 shows Elizabeth switching from the axis line on the right side of her body to the axis line on the left side. Notice how she rides the right axis from extension in frame 1 through the catch in frame 2 and the diagonal in frame 3. In frame 4 she transitions to the axis line on the other side as she begins the

---

### A QUICK CONNECTION

What's the relationship between overwater recovery and axis line balance? A vertical upper arm recovery, with shoulder tucked behind the head, allows you to balance on the axis line. Swimmers who swing the upper arm horizontally are unable to ride the axis line efficiently. A swinging horizontal recovery throws them off balance.

**FIGURE 6.10** Elizabeth rides the right axis line in frames 1–3 and seamlessly switches to the left axis line as she begins to extend her left arm in frames 4–6.

finish phase on the right arm and extends on the left arm. By the time she is fully extending on the left arm, she has seamlessly switched to her left axis line.

As you stroke, feel the balance of riding the axis line. Remember, the line is frontal and runs through the nipple. Don't tip too far, so you can easily switch from one side to the other.

Let's move to the shoulders. As described in Chapter 5, the shoulder on the side of the arm that is extending and catching presses *forward* and juts against the cheek/chin just below the surface. It does not rotate down. Meanwhile, the opposing arm, which is finishing the stroke and lifting from the water, opens up and the shoulder tucks behind the head. The shoulders engage in two separate, independent movements. They are not fused as one unit. One presses forward while the other lifts and pulls toward the spine.

The independent movement of the shoulders is evidenced in Figure 6.11. Notice how Townley's shoulder on the left side, where he is making the catch, remains stable at the side of his cheek/chin while the right shoulder lifts from the water. The right shoulder progressively tucks behind his head as the photo series progresses.

**FIGURE 6.11** Townley's left shoulder remains stable at his cheek/chin as his right shoulder lifts from the water and tucks behind his head. The shoulders engage in independent actions.

**FIGURE 6.12** Peter's hips move together as one unit.

**FIGURE 6.13** The core of Jack's body is ribbon-like as he drives through the water.

The hips are another story. Unlike the shoulders, the hips are fused for the most part. In Figure 6.12, Peter finishes the stroke on his left side (frame 1), with his left hip up and right hip down in the water. When he makes the catch in frame 2, his hips move together to begin rotating the other direction, and by the time he is in the diagonal phase of the stroke in frame 3, his hips are completely neutral in the water. His hips move together as one unit. We can call this "rotation," but keep in mind that more is not better. The degree of hip movement is approximately 30 degrees at the finish of the stroke in frame 1.

In a nutshell, the core is ribbon-like (see Figure 6.13). A swimmer does not move like Frankenstein, rigid and fused. Rather, elite core movement is fluid and quite similar to yoga in water. Various parts of the core do their own thing. One shoulder extends forward, the other shoulder lifts, the hips drive, one up, one down, and the chest finds, balances, and rides on the axis line. It's a gentle game of Twister.

## STROKE TIMING

Elite swimmers may appear to be moving effortlessly at one constant speed, seamlessly switching from one axis line to the other, but in reality, they accelerate and decelerate during the stroke. Forward velocity studies of Olympic swimmers show they reach peak speed at the finish of the pull and then begin to decelerate until the catch is negotiated on the other arm. It makes sense; if neither arm is propulsive, then the water's resistance will slow forward progress. So, the timing between the finish of the stroke with one arm and the catch with the other requires our attention. It also tells us gliding is not a good option for swimmers. If a swimmer finishes the stroke on one side, and glides the other hand/arm in the extension position (delaying making the catch), then deceleration is prolonged.

It's important to learn the stroke timing that minimizes deceleration and gives us a sense of carrying speed through the water. To practice stroke timing, focus on the moment you finish the propulsive pull. When you feel the water leave your hand/arm—when propulsion has ended—don't hesitate, don't glide. Begin "feeling for" the catch on the other hand/arm. The phrase I use at my clinics is "Finish, Feel!" Finish on one side, and then feel for the catch on the other. The "finish-feel" timing is depicted in Townley's stroke in

**FIGURE 6.14** To minimize deceleration, Townley finishes the stroke with his right arm and immediately feels for the catch with his left arm.

Figure 6.14. As his right hand finishes the stroke in frames 1 and 2, he begins feeling for the catch with his left arm.

If you get the gist of the "finish, feel" timing, and of catch details, then you'll master what's called *front quadrant swimming*.

Front quadrant swimming refers to the moment in the stroke cycle that the arms pass by each other, moving in opposite directions. In elite freestyle strokes, this occurs in front of the head—in the front quadrant of the stroke. The pulling arm is making the catch as the other arm recovers in front of the head. Master this timing, and you will minimize deceleration and enjoy the sensation of carrying speed.

To determine if you're a front quadrant swimmer, note where your arms *pass* by each other, not where the pulling arm is when the recovering arm *enters* the water. The distinction is important, because the arms on all elite swimmers, from sprinters to distance swimmers, pass by each other in the front quadrant, but not all elite swimmers' pulling arm is making the catch (in the front quadrant) when the other hand enters the water.

In many mid-distance and distance swimmers, the moment the arms pass by each other *does* correlate with the moment the hand enters the water, as shown in Allison's stroke in Figure 6.15. Here, the propulsive hand is in the thick of the catch when the other hand enters the water. It is considered classic front quadrant swimming. But note this is also the point at which the hands pass by each other—the true definition of front quadrant swimming.

In other elite swimmers' strokes, the pulling arm is in the diagonal phase of the stroke (in the mid to rear quadrant) when the opposing hand enters the water. Viewed from underwater, it appears these elite swimmers are not stroking with front quadrant timing. Such is the case in Figure 6.16. Frames 1 and 2 show Jack and Townley from an underwater perspective. Note that both of their left arms are in the diagonal phase, and still we do not see the right arm entered in the water. Thus, it would appear they are not stroking with front quadrant timing. However, when viewed from an overwater perspective (frames 3 and 4), it's clear that they *do* employ front quadrant timing. The left arm is in the catch phase when the right arm recovers overwater in front of

**FIGURE 6.15** Allison's hands pass by each other as one makes the catch and the other enters the water. This is classic front quadrant technique.

the head. The arms pass by each other in front of their head (overhead). This is elite stroke timing.

If you practice "finish, feel" timing and become a front quadrant swimmer, you will minimize deceleration in your stroke. You will carry momentum and showcase a speed that appears constant and flowing, just like an elite swimmer.

## KICKING

Kicking is a powerful source of propulsion, yet for some swimmers, it is a miserable, thankless exercise. While they enthusiastically pump their legs, they do not move forward, and a few actually move backward. Yes, it is possible to move the wrong direction when kicking!

**FIGURE 6.16** Frames 1 and 2 show both Jack and Townley's propulsive arm in the diagonal phase, and the other hand still has not entered the water. They are swimming with front quadrant timing, however, as evidenced by frames 3 and 4, which show where the hands pass by each other—the left arm in the catch phase and the right arm overwater in front of the head.

Let's look at how to kick properly and how to time it in the freestyle stroke so that you can best utilize this propulsive tool you have at your fingertips—or rather, toe-tips.

As with the arm stroke, we want the foot to travel an ideal distance so water can most effectively be accelerated and *thrown* off the foot at the finish. We need travel distance to do this; therefore, we do not pitter-patter our feet on the water. There are four stages to achieving a meaty, strong kick:

1.  Bend the knee
2.  Flex the hip (press the thigh down in the water)
3.  Straighten the leg
4.  Lift the thigh and lower leg back to the surface

When these four components are carried out in sequential fashion, the kicking action is wave-like and generates great power.

Figure 6.17 shows NCAA champion and Olympic medalist Vladimir Morozov progressing through the four stages of the kick. In frame 1 he bends his right knee, with thighs parallel. In frame 2 he flexes his hip (presses the thigh down), but note that the knee is still bent. It is not until frame 3 that Vladimir straightens his leg to finish the kick, indicating the stages are sequential, not simultaneous. In frame 4 the upper leg recovers by lifting. The leg remains straight as the upper leg lifts. Once the foot reaches hip level, the knee will bend again to start the next kick.

It is important to reiterate two points here, as these are issues common to swimmers who struggle with kicking:

First, for the four kicking stages to be most effective, foot speed must change during the propulsive phases of the kick (steps 2 and 3—hip flexion and leg extension). Some swimmers try too hard at the beginning of the kicking action by extending their leg at the same time they flex the hip. They crash their foot in the water. Foot speed is too fast at this point, and they are unable to accelerate the end of the kick. To properly accelerate, flex the hip, and then extend the leg, as two separate actions. This allows you to build momentum

**FIGURE 6.17** Propulsive kicking entails flexing the hip and then extending the leg, in sequential fashion, not simultaneously.

and feel the sensation of throwing water off your foot at the end of the kick. In Figure 6.18, Jack flexes his hip while keeping his knee bent. Notice in frame 1 that he bends his knee and his thighs are parallel. In frame 2 his knee remains bent as the thigh presses down.

Second, engaging the upper leg is critical. Some swimmers make the error of "kicking from the knees." They flex the hip as shown in frame 2 of Figure 6.17 but fail to lift it back to the surface as shown in frame 4. Their thighs remain low in the water, and they kick from the knees only, bending the knee, then straightening, then re-bending, and so on, never engaging the thigh action in steps 2 and 4. In cases where the force is equal on the up and down kicks of these "knee-kickers," there will be no forward progress, and if the force is greater while bending the knee to bring the foot back to the surface, then the net effect is to move backward in the water.

To prevent swimmers from kicking from the knees, coaches often instruct to "kick from the hips." This does not mean rocking the hips up and down in the water. "Kicking from the hips" refers to hip flexion (step 2) and is very different than rocking the hips. When I see the hips of a swimmer rock up and down, I address the oarlocks concept (see p. 55), because it holds true for kicking just as it does for arm stroking. The feet generate propulsion to move the body forward, and the hips are the oarlocks. The hips must remain stable in the water if propulsion from the leg is to transfer to moving the body forward.

Knowing how to kick with elite technique is one thing, but connecting the kicks with the arm stroke is another.

Elite freestylers incorporate one of three types of kicks: a 2-beat, 4-beat, or 6-beat kick. The number of beats refers to the number of kicks a swimmer makes during *one full stroke cycle*. A 2-beat kicker kicks twice—once with each leg—during a full stroke cycle (a full stroke cycle includes both arms—not just one arm hit). Four-beat kickers incorporate 4 kicks and 6-beat kickers fit in 6 kicks during one full stroke cycle.

**FIGURE 6.18** Jack keeps his knee bent as he flexes his hip (2). Accelerating the kicking action requires that a swimmer progress sequentially through the kicking stages—flexing the hip before extending the leg.

---

### DO YOU CRAMP WHEN KICKING?

Some swimmers experience crippling foot or calf cramps when kicking. This is often a result of trying to point the toes during the kick. Solve the problem by keeping the ankle and foot relaxed—even floppy. You need not point your toes. Once you press your thigh down to initiate the propulsive phase of the kick, the water does the work to point your toes, as seen in frame 2 of Figure 6.17. Some people have more ankle flexibility than others, and so their feet will position slightly better, but even those with less ankle flexibility gain no additional benefit by attempting to point their toes. They are usually only rewarded with a cramp. So, keep your ankles and toes loose and relaxed.

---

I teach only the 6-beat kick, because it is the most propulsive and also because swimmers with 2-beat or 4-beat kicks have them naturally. A 6-beat kick is not natural for all swimmers, and timing the beats is important.

To learn the timing, we have to start somewhere in the stroke cycle. Let's start with the right arm in the extension phase and go beat to beat:

**Beat 1:** When the right arm extends, the left leg kicks down.
**Beat 2:** When the right arm catches, the right leg kicks down.
**Beat 3:** When the right arm is in the diagonal phase, the left leg kicks down.
**Beat 4:** When the right arm finishes the stroke, the right leg kicks down.
**Beat 5:** When the right arm recovers, the left leg kicks down.
**Beat 6:** When the right arm enters the water, the right leg kicks down.

In sum, a swimmer kicks once during each propulsive phase on each arm—the catch, diagonal, and finish—so 3 beats of the kick occur as each arm pulls.

Feeling every beat of the 6-beat kick in a stroke cycle is difficult; it happens too fast. The good news is that there is an easy way to learn the timing. The cue is *kick-catch*! If you concentrate on that particular beat—kicking down on the same side of the arm that is making the catch, you will hit every beat thereafter.

Figure 6.19 shows Elizabeth incorporating 6-beat kick timing. In frame 1 she extends her right arm and kicks down with her left leg. Next comes the kick-catch beat, shown in frames 2–4. Elizabeth kicks down with her right leg as she makes the catch with her right arm. The motion happens quickly, yet it takes 3 frames to capture from beginning to end. She starts the kick as she starts the catch (frame 2), and she finishes the kick as she finishes the catch (frame 4). Frame 5 shows Elizabeth kick down with her left leg as she navigates the diagonal phase of the stroke, and in frame 6 she kicks down with her right leg as she finishes the stroke.

The kick timing we see in Elizabeth's stroke is not haphazard. If you incorporate a well-timed 6-beat kick into your freestyle stroke you will feel propulsive assistance in the form of rear-wheel drive!

## BREATHING

With the exception of the 50 Freestyle in competition, during which athletes breathe only once or twice during the entire race, elite swimmers breathe every 1–2 full stroke cycles. Velocity dips during strokes when an athlete takes a breath, but the alternative is worse—not enough oxygen being delivered to the muscles.

Champions Katie Ledecky and Michael Phelps breathe every stroke cycle, but they minimize the negative impact to their velocity by ensuring they do two things really well: They return their head to the water and get balanced on the axis line while making the catch, before pulling through.

To take a breath, a swimmer not only turns the head to the side but also rotates the body further to the side than on the non-breathing strokes. This slightly off-balance rotation is necessary to get the breath. The best of the best do something very sophisticated though. After they take in air, they turn their head back into the water and re-balance on the axis line while feeling for the catch. Other swimmers pull through while they're still tipped slightly off balance, which causes a loss of distance traveled on that arm stroke. It may be a minimal loss on one given stroke, but the strokes add up over the course of a race.

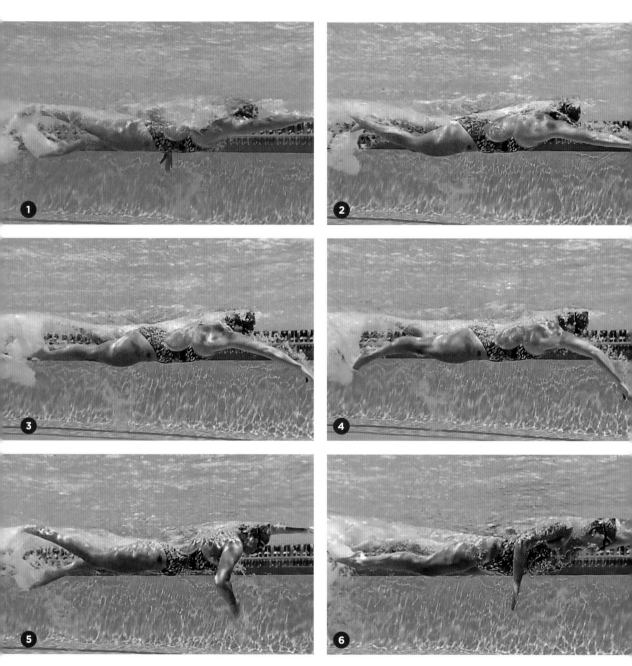

**FIGURE 6.19** A 6-beat kick is timed such that one beat occurs during each of the propulsive phases of the pull on each arm.

Figure 6.20 shows elite breathing technique. Townley turns his head and body to the side to take a breath in frame 1. In frames 2–3 he begins to return his head to the water and re-balance on the axis line as he starts feeling for the catch. By frame 4, when he has made the catch, his head is completely back in the water, and he is fully balanced on the right axis line. The propulsive phases of his pull take place while he is balanced just where he should be.

Practice this feature of elite breathing technique, and you may find yourself among the best of the best.

## HEAD AND BODY POSITION

When it comes to head position, your neck should be neutral so that you break the water at the crown of your head.

As for body position, your body should be horizontal (in other words, your legs should not drag through the water). If you generate propulsion, you'll be horizontal.

## MEANINGFUL PRACTICE

Do you see why you needed a strong Italian roast to get through the past few chapters? There's a lot to absorb. When swimmers feel overwhelmed by the details, I remind them this is what makes practice meaningful and engaging. All complex activities take time to master. Don't feel that you need to conquer everything in a weekend. Enjoy the intrinsic rewards that come along with chipping away at a complex activity.

The process of building the stroke is both a puzzle and an art. You are at liberty to work on any part of the technique you wish at any given moment. All dedicated effort—whether on vital or nonvital elements—will make you a better swimmer. You truly are your own best coach. If something you read here made you shout, "Ah-ha! That may be the cause my shoulder pain," then I suggest working on that part of the stroke before anything else. Or, if you've always wanted to improve your kick, then you could focus primarily on that

**FIGURE 6.20** After taking a breath, Townley returns his head to the water and rebalances on the axis line as he makes the catch.

aspect of freestyle for weeks. I salute any deliberate purposeful practice. More than anything, I want you to enjoy your time in the water, so if working on axis line balance makes swimming most interesting and fun on any given day, then work on axis line balance. The next chapter provides a smorgasbord of drills and exercises that work every part of the stroke, vital and nonvital.

I've made the claim that pull mechanics are the vital elements of the stroke, and I stand by that. When I coach swimmers I spend most of the time on the propulsive phases of the pull, simply because it requires time to go through the details. Other parts of the stroke are learned much more quickly. It gets tiring mentally for swimmers to stay focused on the details of the pull, so after 10–15 minutes of intense work there, I'll give the arms a break and have swimmers think about something else for a set or two, and then go back to pull mechanics.

When you work on the nonvital elements, place your focus fully on them. Don't worry about the pull when you drill those. If you're trying to think of everything at once, you'll be thinking of nothing at all.

Ultimately, everything ties together. Enjoy the moments when you connect the dots. It will happen. Patience in developing the full scope of the stroke is the key.

# 7

# DEVELOPING
# THE FREESTYLE STROKE

## DRILLS & EXERCISES

**"EFFICIENT" IS A WORD I HEAR** often from swimmers and triathletes at my clinics. They sign up for the clinic because they want to become "efficient" with their swimming. When pressed to elaborate, they say they hope to learn a technique that will make them fast (or at least faster) with minimal energy output. Good swimmers make swimming look easy as they glide effortlessly through the water, they say, and "efficient" best captures this observation. Being efficient therefore is strongly associated with the idea of minimal output.

When a word becomes popular I get curious and look at it more closely. Turns out, the word "efficient" comes from "effect"—to accomplish, to cause, to make, as in to make an outcome. Synonyms include *businesslike, productive, disciplined*, and *practiced*. Additional synonyms are *dynamic, powerful, energetic, tough*, and *skilled*. I looked through every thesaurus and could not find any synonyms relating to minimal output such as "easy, simple, kicked-back, and relaxed."

In this chapter, the goal is to help you make an outcome—that is, to become efficient with your swimming. This involves an element of practice and production. There's a toughness component to it too. Don't let this deter you. I tried to find the word "fun" under the list of synonyms for "efficient," and just like "easy," it wasn't there, but trust me on this—there is a fun factor. Maybe not at first when your lats and deltoids are on fire, but soon you'll see that getting stronger and faster is synonymous with fun.

This chapter details in-water drills and an out-of-water exercise that build agility, muscle memory, muscle tone, and endurance in your stroke. You will focus on form, mechanics, and technique when you do these. Chapter 8 addresses rate of turnover, and that is when we can apply the "dynamic and energetic" elements of "efficiency" to our swimming. Those are only effective, however, if the foundation of form is first established.

Let's go have fun!

## IN-WATER DRILLS

As a crucial part of technique training, in-water drills should be incorporated into every workout. I like to drill during my warm-up, but I also add short drill sets to the middle of my workout for recovery, a change of pace, and a sharpening of technique.

The purpose of in-water drills is to emphasize one or more aspects of the stroke. They often overdo certain motions to drive home a point, and in the process, part of the stroke may be sacrificed. For this reason, it is important to know why you're doing each drill, what you ultimately want to adopt into your regular stroke, and—perhaps as important—what you should not adopt.

This chapter presents eight drills. Don't do every one in every workout! Pick a few you feel will best compliment your session; 200–300 meters of each will suffice (although 400–500 meters is fine too). I usually mix drills with swimming. For instance, in warm-up, I will do 8 × 50, with the first 25 being drill, the second 25 swim. Then, during the middle of a workout, when I'm tired, I'll throw in 4–8 lengths of a drill, usually in 25-meter increments. It's perfectly acceptable and beneficial to do 100–300 meters straight through of a drill as well. Guide yourself based on what you feel you need.

## STREAMLINING

Whether drilling or swimming, be sure to streamline off every wall at practice. Streamlining is the best way to build tone in your core muscles. It's especially good training for the muscles surrounding the scapula to gain the range of motion that is necessary to extend the arms overhead for the catch. Many triathletes think they shouldn't streamline since they race in open water and do not push off walls; however, they still need to streamline when practicing in the pool to develop mobility in the scapula region (and to analyze their performance data, as explained in the next chapter).

To do a great streamline, push off at a depth of 2–3 feet underwater for approximately 2 seconds before surfacing to stroke. With arms overhead, place one hand on top of the other, and clasp the thumb from the top hand around the outside edge of the bottom hand to prevent the hands from separating, as the photo of Margaret Kelly shows.

Squeeze your arms together behind your ears, elbows locked. You will feel tension tugging your arms to pull them apart, but the clasped thumb prevents them from separating. Lengthen the muscles in the front and back of your core, especially concentrating on the scapular region. Press your scapula forward so your shoulders jut against the base of your skull. As we see in Margaret's technique, there should be no gap between the shoulders and head. We can see every muscle in Margaret's back and shoulders engaged. Who would pass up an opportunity for such a great workout off every wall? It's yoga in water.

## 1. SCULLING IN THE CATCH POSITION

Sculling is a slow moving drill, so slow that it appears not much work is being done, but it's one elite swimmers cherish. You can scull in a variety of positions—on your stomach, back, or vertically (treading water is a sculling action), with one arm or both, above the head or under the body. My favorite way is in the catch position, because it simulates the actual movement the hand/arm makes during that phase of the stroke. During the catch, an elite swimmer feels the water in every direction *other than pushing back*, and the main benefit derived from sculling is learning what it's like to feel the water laterally and at the proper depth. There is no back pressing component to sculling.

### Instructions

Push off the wall in a streamlined position, then surface, keeping both arms in front of your head. Reach your upper arms forward by lengthening the muscles that attach to your scapula. Sweep your upper arms 4–8 inches (1–2 hand widths) wide of shoulder width, bend your elbows, and medially rotate your upper arm. Hold your upper arms in this position for the duration of the drill.

Position your head as if swimming normally—face in the water, neck neutral. Lift the head when you need a breath, then put your face back in the water.

Working from your forearms, press your palms out, sweeping away from each other (outsweep) until they reach the same width as your elbows, as shown in frames 1–3 of Figure 7.1. After the outsweep, switch direction for the insweep. Press your palms toward each other until they nearly touch in front of your shoulders (frames 4–6). Continue sweeping out and in for the length of the pool. As you work the in-and-out sculling motions, be sure your upper arm remains stable in the catch position the entire time. This drill develops great muscle tone in the arms and back, even though we move at a snail's pace.

You may kick lightly to help with forward movement, but notice how, if you stop kicking, the sculling motion will move you forward—it's slow going, but you'll get there.

**FIGURE 7.1** When sculling in the catch position, the palms press out (1–3), then in (4–6). There is no back-pressing component to sculling.

### Reminders and Pointers

**Elbow depth.** Your elbow should be 3–10 inches below the surface of the water; find the depth that works best for you. That is the depth you ultimately want to incorporate in your stroke. The key is to feel like you can function athletically. Don't hold your elbow higher if it makes you too rigid.

**Hand depth.** Your hands should scull at a depth approximately 2 feet deep. Become familiar feeling the water with your palms at that depth since this is where elite swimmers' hands ultimately make the catch.

**Hand speed cues.** By moving your hands/forearms laterally while overhead during this drill (and not pressing back), you are keying in on what it means to control your hand speed during this early phase of the stroke. You are laying the foundation for a great "feel" for water.

### What Not to Adopt

Sculling emphasizes *lateral* hand/arm movements. Remember that in the actual swim stroke, *after* the catch phase, lateral movements are not as dominant as back-pressing movements. Therefore, once you've made the catch, feel some lateral movement in the stroke but primarily feel back-pressing action.

Also remember that the medial rotation of the upper arm that is held during the entirety of this drill is part of the catch phase of the stroke only. When you swim, be sure you don't hold the medial rotation as you transition to the diagonal phase.

## 2. ONE-ARM STROKING

One-arm stroking places a laser focus on the mechanics of one arm without worrying about the arm on the other side. In this drill, one arm remains stationary, either at your side or in front of you in the extended position, as the other arm strokes. You can think about any of the propulsive phases of the pull, the non-propulsive phases, axis line balance, or kick timing when you do this drill, but in this book I'm going to highlight how you can work on elite breathing technique.

## Instructions

To work on elite breathing, do this drill with your nonstroking arm at your side and breathe to that nonworking side every stroke. The goal is to get your head back in the water and return to the axis line on the stroking side as you make the catch. In the actual swim stroke, many swimmers lose forward momentum/velocity when they take a breath because they return the head to the water too late and do not balance on the axis line soon enough.

**FIGURE 7.2** Townley takes a breath (1) and then gets his head back in the water and balances on the axis line as he makes the catch (2 and 3). This ensures he will get the most from his stroke as he pulls through (4).

Figure 7.2 shows Townley doing a one-arm stroke with his arm at his side and taking a breath. He breathes to the left (his nonworking side) in frame 1 as his right arm extends. In frames 2 and 3 he gets his head back in the water and balances on the axis line on the right side of his body as he makes the catch. This is the key to elite breathing. By tending to these details he is able to better maintain speed (e.g., minimize the negative effects of taking a breath) as he pulls through in frame 4.

Gains you make toward mastering this elite-level breathing will add up to a big difference in your performance.

### Reminders and Pointers

**Breathe to the correct side.** When doing this drill with your nonworking arm at your side, breathe to that side. If you choose at times to do this drill with your nonworking arm extended in front of you (to work on mechanics other than breathing technique), then take your breath to the side of the arm that is stroking.

**Kick.** A strong supporting 6-beat kick helps maintain forward velocity while the stroking arm navigates the nonpropulsive phases. You can get a great kick workout while doing one-arm drills!

### What Not to Adopt

You're not at risk for adopting any bad habits with this drill, unless of course you forget to use both arms when you swim.

### 3. ONE-ARM WITH KICKBOARD

This drill is very similar to the one-arm stroke drill. We stroke with one arm only, but in this version the nonstroking arm is extended and held stationary on top of a kickboard, and the head is held out of water. This is one of my go-to drills when I want to build strength in my core and arms. You can work all phases of the arm stroke—propulsive and nonpropulsive—during this drill. It is also fantastic for feeling axis line balance and *kick-catch* timing.

## Instructions

Place your nonstroking hand flat on top of the middle of a kickboard and keep your head out of water. Look straight ahead and stroke with the working hand/arm.

Figure 7.3 shows Jack doing the drill. His head is out of water, and he looks forward.

## Reminders and Pointers

**Look straight ahead, with your head out of water.** As swimmers fatigue on this drill, they tend to throw their head to the side and get sloppy with their stroking motion. Looking straight ahead forces you to strengthen your core, and you can watch your hand/arm make the catch in front of you.

**Incorporate hand speed change.** This drill is physically demanding, so some swimmers go into survival mode, rushing through the stroking motion, especially the catch phase. Be patient and attend to the details of the catch, including slower hand speed as you navigate width and depth. Build hand speed from there. You'll know you're doing this drill with elite technique when your body and the kickboard surges forward on the back half of the propulsive pull—namely at the finish phase.

**FIGURE 7.3** During the one-arm with kickboard drill, notice that Jack's head is out of the water and he looks straight ahead.

**Train the overwater phases of the stroke.** Figure 7.3 captures Jack in the overwater recovery phase of the stroke. This drill is ideal for training the muscle agility and endurance for lifting the upper arm to a vertical position before recovering the hand forward. Notice in frames 1 and 2 that Jack's hand does not recover forward. Rather, the upper arm lifts from the water and the hand remains near the hip. Once the vertical upper arm position is established in frame 2, Jack's hand recovers forward, as shown in frame 3.

Also remember from Chapter 6 that the beginning of the overwater recovery phase of the stroke is synched with the catch on the other arm; thus, hand speed is slow during these moments. By resisting the urge to bring the hand forward as you establish the vertical upper arm position during the first part of the overwater recovery, you achieve the "slower" hand speed that leads to elite stroking rhythm.

### What Not to Adopt

Though the amazing Johnny Weissmuller boasted world-record times in the 1920s with his head out of water, please do not swim with yours out of water. You'll be faster with it in the water.

### 4. TARZAN DRILL

This drill simulates Johnny Weissmuller's competitive swim stroke. It's named Tarzan because Johnny played Tarzan in the movies after retiring from competitive swimming. This drill is great for building catch mechanics and a propulsive pull, but I especially like that it prevents overrotation. Because Johnny kept his head out of the water, looking straight ahead, we do the same during this drill, which keeps us balanced on the axis line. If a swimmer overrotates during this drill, the head thrashes to the side and is very difficult to keep above water.

### Instructions

Swim a normal freestyle stroke but with your head above water, looking straight ahead the entire time.

Note in Figure 7.4 how Peter keeps his head above water and looks straight ahead. This is great training for working catch mechanics and balancing on the axis line.

### Reminders and Pointers

**Feel the axis line.** Take note of how you ride the front of your rib cage on the right side of your body when your right arm extends and catches and then easily switch to the left axis line when the left arm enters and catches.

**Work the rate of turnover.** Because the Tarzan drill encourages you to ride the axis line properly, you are in prime position to pick up your rate of turnover.

**Enjoy building strength in your core and shoulders.** This drill is challenging because of the head-out-of-water element. Embrace the sensation of fatigue in the upper half of your body, knowing you're building Tarzan strength.

### What Not to Adopt

As with the one-arm with kickboard drill, when it comes to your real stroke, keep that head in the water. You can adopt everything else though!

**FIGURE 7.4** During the Tarzan drill, keep your head above water and look straight ahead. This allows you to balance and ride the axis line with elite technique.

## 5. CATCH-LIFT DRILL

Elite mechanics can be watered down if hand speed change is not incorporated into the technique (see Chapter 5). This drill teaches the sensation of slower hand speed during the two moments in the stroke cycle that require patience. Keep in mind, however, that the instruction to implement slower hand speed does not suggest passively gliding or stopping the hand(s) from moving. Rather, it entails moving the hand(s) in directions other than forward/back.

### Instructions

Position horizontally in the water as if swimming. With one hand extended overhead directly in front of your shoulder, and the other near your hip as if it has just finished the propulsive pull, begin to kick. The kick is your primary source of propulsion during this drill. As you kick the length of the pool, simultaneously navigate depth and width for the catch on the front arm, and lift the elbow up and out the water with the back arm. That is the drill: to catch on one arm, and lift the other. Neither hand/arm moves forward or back during their respective actions. Once you have made the catch and lifted, return the arms to their original positions (with the front arm extended and the back hand next to the hip). Repeat the catch-lift action 2–3 times on one side, and then pull through and switch sides to practice the action 2–3 times before switching again.

In Figure 7.5, I showcase the drill. In frame 1 my front hand/arm is in extension position and my rear hand is positioned near the hip, simulating the finish moment of the stroke. In frame 2 my front hand navigates width and depth to make the catch while my rear hand/arm lifts up from the water. Notice how neither hand/arm moves forward or backward during these moments in the stroke cycle. This is how hand speed is controlled during these two critical moments of the arm stroking motion.

### Reminders and Pointers

**Be patient.** Remember that kicking is your primary source of propulsion during this drill, except when you pull through to switch sides, so it's slow moving. Resist the urge to do this drill quickly. Speed is not the point.

**FIGURE 7.5** Begin the catch-lift drill with one hand extended in front of the shoulder and the other next to the hip (1), and then navigate width and depth for the catch on the front hand as you lift the back hand from the water (2). Neither hand moves forward or back.

**Believe.** Sophisticated sport movement involves impulse and rhythm—and impulse and rhythm are based on speed change, also known as acceleration. Believe in the moments when hand speed slows. Believe in the science of acceleration. Hand speed must *change* for water to be accelerated back, which is a swimmer's source of propulsion. This drill challenges you to discover how you can move on dimensions other than fore-aft in our beautiful sport to accomplish maximal propulsion.

### What Not to Adopt

This drill trains a very specific moment in the stroke cycle, and you can and should adopt 100 percent of the elements it teaches.

## 6. SUPERMAN DRILL

Superman incorporates multiple stroking features in a snapshot moment. It trains balancing on the axis line, front quadrant stroke timing, catch mechanics, and the vertical upper arm recovery position. And because your only source of propulsion is kicking, you get in a great kick workout. You also learn buoyancy during this drill. Many athletes sink when first trying Superman. If this happens to you, keep at it. You'll learn how to hold air in your lungs and stay on top of the water after a few attempts.

### Instructions

Push off the wall in a streamline position. Upon surfacing, set one arm in the catch position and pull through with the other arm, but stop the pulling arm when it reaches the point in the overwater recovery just before entry; it will be overwater and in front of your head. Hold it there.

Superman is like a game of "statue." Set the position and do not move, except to kick (your only source of propulsion). Both arms should be overhead: one in the water in the catch position, and the other above water about to enter. This is the front quadrant timing moment in the stroke cycle reviewed in the previous chapter.

In addition to holding your arms in their very specific positions, concentrate on balancing your body on the axis line. Ride the front of your rib cage on the same side of the arm that is in the catch position.

Figure 7.6, frame 1, shows Jack doing the Superman drill. Notice how he is in the catch position with his right arm and is balanced on the axis line on the right side of his body. Frame 2 captures this moment in the stroke as Jack swims freestyle. The drill requires balance and strength from both the catching arm and the overwater arm.

### Reminders and Pointers

**Breathing.** To breathe during Superman, turn your head toward the side of the arm that is out of the water, get a breath, and then get your head back in the water, all while holding the Superman position. If this feels too difficult at first,

**FIGURE 7.6** The Superman drill trains the moment in the stroke cycle when both arms are overhead—one in water and the other above water, with the swimmer balanced on the axis line (1). Frame 2 captures this same moment in Jack's actual stroke cycle.

then hold your breath in the position for 10 seconds and swim the rest of the length for recovery, breathing as often as you like. As you build strength and endurance for the drill, you will be able to do a full length of the pool, turning your head for breath when you need it.

**Resistance.** You should feel resistance on the forearm that is in the catch position. A natural instinct is to avoid resistance and therefore to straighten that arm and slipstream it through the water. Do not do that. We are drilling a specific moment in the stroke cycle, and it's not a race. Keep the arm in the catch position, which means the forearm is completely vertical and encountering a great deal of resistance. Study the position of the arm that is catching in frame 1 of Figure 7.6 to ensure you attend to this detail.

**Hold that elbow up.** Maintain a strong vertical upper arm position with the arm that is out of the water. Don't lay it on the surface as if it's napping. Your fingertips can nearly touch the water surface, but not the elbow.

The key to benefiting from this drill is to be very particular about the positions of both the arms and your body. I'd rather you hold these positions correctly for a ⅓ or ½ length, rather than going into survival mode, dropping the elbow or tipping on your side, in order to make a full length of the pool. Rest when you repeat this drill so that you do it correctly each time.

**Superman 2.0.** This version incorporates sculling. To add this feature, scull three times back and forth with the hand that is in the catch position, then pull through and set the Superman position on the other side. Scull three times with that hand/arm, and then switch again. Reset the Superman position quickly when you switch sides. This version also works elite breathing mechanics. After sculling three times and then pulling through, take a breath to the side that is pulling, then get your head back in the water as you set the catch for the Superman position on the other arm.

### What Not to Adopt

Superman trains a snapshot moment of the stroke. Every part of the body is set in the position you want to be in when you pass through this moment during the stroke cycle. Nothing is overexaggerated or sacrificed, so adopt everything!

### 7. SHARK FIN

The shark fin drill is all about the finish of the stroke. First and foremost, it trains hand speed acceleration. Second, it trains agility in the chest/shoulder region so the scapula packs in toward the midline of the body during the finish.

### Instructions

Place a kickboard between your thighs just as you would a pull buoy, ensuring that the majority of the board sticks out behind your legs. Swim normal freestyle, with the board sticking out of the water as you swim. As you finish each stroke and your hand/arm exits the water, hit the kickboard with that hand before going into the overwater recovery phase of the stroke. To make contact with the board, you will feel your scapula pack in, which pulls your shoulder partly behind your head, as described in Chapter 6. Reaching the board also requires acceleration from the hand. The board remains elusive if you do not have a dynamic snap to the finishing moment.

Figure 7.7 shows Townley doing the shark fin drill. With a kickboard between his legs he swims normal freestyle and finishes the stroke with his left arm (frame 1). To reach the kickboard for the hit (frame 2), he pulls his scapula toward the midline of his body. Notice the difference in shoulder position between frames 1 and 2. In frame 1 his shoulder is to the side of his head, and in frame 2 his shoulder pulls toward the midline of his body to stack partly behind his head. Shark fin develops the scapular mobility and strength needed for this aspect of the finishing action.

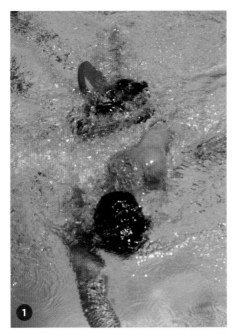

**FIGURE 7.7** To reach the kickboard, Townley must accelerate his hand and pull his scapula toward the midline of his body.

### Reminders and Pointers

**Extended arm.** When you hit the board with one hand, your other arm should be fully extended in front of your shoulder, as in frame 2. This simulates elite technique. After the hit, begin to feel for the catch on the other arm. In this way, the shark fin drill can also be used to learn the "finish-feel" timing outlined in Chapter 6.

**Keep a regular stroking tempo.** Give the board a quick tap and keep stroking. Do not kick. Your legs are fully tasked with holding the board between your thighs. When you first try shark fin, the kickboard may pop out from between your legs, but soon you'll learn how to hold it there. Turning at the end of each length is a challenge too, but you can even do a flip turn while keeping the board in place.

**Feel the flick.** Hand acceleration is not a muscular effort; it is a dynamic, snappy effort in which we feel water get thrown off our hand. It is often referred to as a "flick" at the finish of the stroke. The "flick" is the acceleration factor. Shark fin drill gives us insight into the finishing flick and how this differs from trying to muscle water back. You'll be a step closer to developing an elite feel for the water if you incorporate this drill into your workouts occasionally.

### What Not to Adopt

Reaching back to hit the board requires that you throw your hand over your legs, toward the midline of your body. This is an overexaggeration of the scapular action. In the actual swim stroke, no elite athlete throws the hand over the legs. The hand lifts directly up from the position where it finished alongside the hip. Therefore, do not adopt this exaggerated action. Instead, feel how you have more range of motion and agility for the perfect amount of opening up the chest/shoulder at the finish.

Also, in this drill, you straighten your arm to reach the kickboard. Do not adopt this into your regular stroke. Elite swimmers keep their elbow bent as they finish and lift the arm from the water.

Figure 7.8 shows a side-by-side comparison of Townley doing the shark fin drill (frame 1) and swimming freestyle as he normally does (frame 2). The comparison highlights what to adopt from the drill as well as what not to adopt. Notice the scapular movement in both photos, and the extension of the right arm in both photos. These are two features to take from the drill. However, note the differences as well. Townley's elbow is bent for the finish in frame 2 and straightened for shark fin. Also, he does not throw his hand over his legs when he swims. Therefore, a straight-arm finish and throwing the hand over the legs are two things we do not want to adopt from this drill.

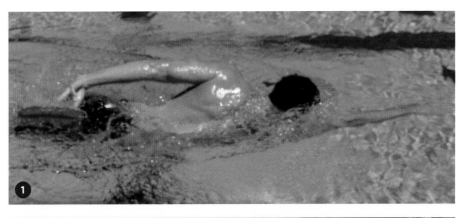

**FIGURE 7.8** Note the similarities and differences in Townley's technique in this side-by-side comparison of him doing the shark fin drill (1) and swimming freestyle as he normally does (2).

## 8. FINGERTIP DRAG

This drill is both simple and relaxing. Try it when you've had a hard day and wouldn't mind if something beneficial for you is also easy. You've probably done the fingertip drag before, but you may well have been concentrating on the wrong part of your stroke. Many people think this drill is about training the lower arm during the overwater recovery phase of the stroke. The drill's name makes us think it's about our fingertips recovering near the surface of the water, with forearm dangling, but it's not. Fingertip drag drill is about the *upper arm*. It trains the vertical upper arm position highlighted in Chapter 6. You'll build strength in the rear deltoid and around the scapula with this one, but it won't be exhausting or difficult, I promise.

### Instructions

Swim freestyle, and as you finish the stroke and lift your hand from the water, keep your fingertips touching the surface of the water, from the finish near your hip through the entire overwater recovery phase to the entry in front of your head.

Figure 7.9 shows Townley doing the fingertip drag drill. From the finish near his hip in frame 1, through to the entry in front of his shoulder in frame 6, he drags his fingertips along the surface of the water. But the drill is not about those fingertips. Study the position of his upper arm. By dragging his fingertips, his upper arm recovers over the water in vertical fashion, not a horizontal swinging fashion.

### Reminders and Pointers

**Take it easy.** Focus on the sensations of engaging your scapula and rear deltoid as you do this drill. Go as slow and easy as you want. You get equal benefit in terms of building strength at any speed.

**Enjoy a perfect entry.** A vertical upper arm during the overwater recovery phase of the stroke sets up a swimmer for a perfect entry in front of the shoulder. You can even add a little work on the elbow "splash" into the water if you want (see Chapter 6).

**FIGURE 7.9** Fingertip drag drill trains upper arm mechanics for the overwater recovery phase of the stroke.

**Remember that this drill trains upper, not lower, arm mechanics.** Figure 7.10 shows Townley doing the drill alongside his actual swim stroke. While the lower arm is in a slightly different position during the drill compared to swimming, the upper arm is in an identical position in both frames.

### What Not to Adopt

The common factor among elite swimmers' overwater recoveries is the upper arm position. The lower arm position varies, however, from a dangling forearm to a hand and forearm held higher. Some elite swimmers even hold their

**FIGURE 7.10** The position of Townley's upper arm during fingertip drag drill (1 and 2) is identical to that of his actual swim stroke (3 and 4).

hand above their elbow in a "straight-arm" recovery fashion. In this drill you may find that you prefer the dangling forearm position. If so, then adopt that. If that position strains your shoulder or doesn't allow you to feel balanced with the weight of your arm as it recovers, then do not adopt the dangling forearm aspect of this drill. When you swim, hold your lower arm in the position that is most comfortable for you and where you can best relax your hand.

## OUT-OF-WATER EXERCISE

Elite swim technique can be navigated without difficulty for a stroke or two, or even for 50 to 100 meters of easy swimming, but what happens 1,200 meters into a workout or 120 meters into a 200-meter race? Form deteriorates on any swimmer who does not remain focused on sensations of propulsion and/or who does not train the muscle endurance necessary to maintain the form.

Drills and focused regular swimming build muscle memory and strength for a propulsive swim stroke, but an out-of-water program accelerates and fortifies this process. For this reason, the majority of elite swimmers add a strength program to their training, including weight room exercises. I am a proponent of weight lifting and general strength exercises for swimming (cycling and running too). Unfortunately, there are no machines that fully simulate the unique movements of the swim stroke, especially the rotational movements of the upper arm. We can train the deltoids, triceps, and lats with various exercises, but not in the way we actually pull.

---

### A NOTE TO NEW SWIMMERS

Chapter 3 includes a note to new swimmers who may need to work first on becoming comfortable with the water but who can still make great strides on the pull doing dry-land exercises. I was referring to tubing and Halo bench work; the exercises outlined here are intended as much for you as they are for the seasoned swimmer who has competed for decades.

## TUBING: MY SECRET TRAINING WEAPON

The Halo™ swim training bench and tubing were specifically designed to train the underwater pull path. Because the exercise is done out of water, athletes can pause in the middle of a pull and check their arm, hand, and shoulder positions. If they are not within the elite parameters described, then they can adjust. Athletes can also hold certain positions for 20-second increments to sear in the endurance for each phase of the stroke. Over time, elite muscle memory will develop and translate directly to their stroke in the water. A 15-minute tubing workout three times per week builds endurance for sustaining elite technique throughout a workout and a race.

Make tubing a part of your general strength program. If you are limited on time, the end of this chapter provides ideas on how to fit tubing into an already busy day.

### Instructions

The details of the propulsive pull path described in Chapter 5 should be mimicked with tubing (with exception of the finish phase, explained in the following pages). This can be done with tubing alone or with a Halo bench and template system. The Halo bench/template positions you horizontally as you would be swimming, and together they guide you through the pull path to ensure you navigate particular details of the stroke—but if you concentrate on these details without the guidance of the template, the workout is just as beneficial.

The photos and instructions in the upcoming section show the exercise with the bench and template. To do the exercise with tubing only, simply bend at the waist so your upper body is horizontal (ensure a healthy back posture).

Attach tubing to any anchored pole at the pool, such as a ladder, diving board, or backstroke flagpole. It can also be attached to door handles at home or in a hotel room.

Place the Halo bench approximately 6 feet away from the point at which the tubing is attached, so there is no slack in the tubing when you extend your arms forward. Lay on your stomach on the bench, so you are in a horizontal position just as you would be when swimming.

### Extension

Start with the arm extended directly in front of your shoulder (Figure 7.11). Train scapular mobility during this phase by pushing your scapula forward. Tension from the tubing encourages extension by pulling your arm forward. Take advantage of this feature, as it helps you gain range of motion in your scapular region and shoulders.

### The Catch

The Halo template is designed with a catch zone. The catch zone requires that you keep your upper arm/elbow *extended* forward while

**FIGURE 7.11** Extend with a straight arm directly in front of shoulder.

your hand and forearm navigates width and depth. If you are new to Halo tubing, be sure to pause at the catch (Figure 7.12) and ensure the following:

- Upper arm is medially rotated, elbow directing up.
- Your elbow and hand are 1–2 hand widths wider than your shoulder. To find your ideal width, note the sensation of the tendons and ligaments inside your shoulder joint. Do they feel lined up? If they feel out of line, then adjust the width of your catch in or out slightly until they feel in alignment.
- Elbow is bent approximately 90 degrees, directing your hand 1–2 feet deeper than it was at extension.
- Reach with your upper arm as you bend your elbow. Don't pull your upper arm back during this phase. Figure 7.13 shows, from a profile view, how the Halo template guides you to make an elite "overhead" catch.

**FIGURE 7.12** Tubing teaches and strengthens an athlete for elite stroking mechanics, including the catch.

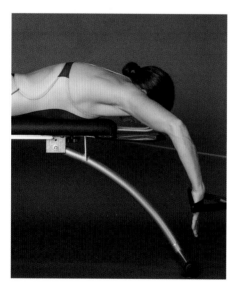

**FIGURE 7.13** Whether training on tubing or swimming, keep the elbow in front of the head while bending the arm for the catch.

If you hold this static catch position for 20-second increments, you'll get a great workout in your core, arms, and the muscles surrounding your scapula!

### The Diagonal

Once you've established the catch, you can begin to press back. Keep pressure against the paddle as you un-rotate your upper arm. The template tapers in to guide your hand/arm in as it presses back. Follow the template. Pause when you feel you are in the thick of the diagonal phase. Figures 7.14 and 7.15 show these important indications that you are doing the exercise correctly:

- Your hand is under your body. This results from un-rotating the upper arm, not from increasing elbow bend. Check to see that your elbow bend is the same now as it was during the catch.
- Upper arm is angled approximately 45 degrees in relation to the imaginary water surface. It should not be parallel with the ground (if it is, then your hand is wide of your body, not under it as it should be, and you are at risk of shoulder injury).
- Your hand is lined up with your elbow/forearm and upper arm, acting as one paddle pressing back. The diagonal phase of the stroke is when swimmers are most likely to "drop" their elbow on the fore-aft dimension. Note in Figure 7.15 how hand, forearm, and upper arm all line up during this mid-phase of the pull. Your rear deltoid gets a great workout holding this position on tubing.
- Your shoulder is shrugged near your cheek/chin, indicating you've maintained stable oarlocks.

As with the catch, you could hold this static position for 20-second increments and gain great muscle memory and endurance for a more propulsive swim stroke.

### The Finish

The finish of the stroke on tubing is the only phase that does not fully simulate what elite swimmers do in the water. To finish on tubing: Extend/straighten

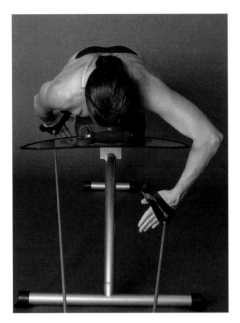 

**FIGURE 7.14** Simulate the mechanics of the diagonal phase of the stroke when training on tubing.

**FIGURE 7.15** When training the diagonal phase of the stroke on tubing, ensure that you maintain oarlocks as your upper arm, forearm, and hand line up on the fore-aft dimension.

the arms fully toward your hips. While the straightened arm position is not what we want to adopt and translate in the water, the benefit of this is a great strength workout for the triceps in your upper arm.

### The Recovery

The Halo bench and tubing trains the underwater propulsive phases of the arm stroke only. At no time during this exercise should you lift your arm above your body, (simulating the overwater recovery phase of the stroke). Doing so risks the tubing pulling your arm forward suddenly. After finishing with your hand next to your hip, recover directly forward, with your hand below you, closer to the ground.

### Reminders and Pointers

**Pull options.** You may pull both arms simultaneously (butterfly pulls) or alternate one arm at a time (freestyle pulls), as shown in Figure 7.16 The mechanics are the same whichever you choose.

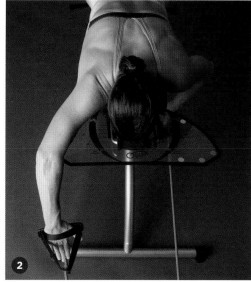

**FIGURE 7.16** Pull with two arms (butterfly pulls—1), or alternate one arm at a time (freestyle pulls—2). The mechanics are the same.

**Train your tempo for a specific race.** Tubing should first be used to establish correct mechanics. Once the pattern becomes natural, a swimmer can pull on tubing at a faster rate, simulating a desired race tempo. The next chapter highlights elite rates of turnover for various race distances and helps you calculate your rate. Once you know your rate, it can be converted to the number of pulls per minute you should target on tubing.

**An exercise that isolates the triceps will strengthen your upper arm.** The triceps isolation is simply the finish phase of the tubing exercise. Figure 7.17 shows the exercise.

The upper arm remains stable against your side as you bend your elbow to 90 degrees, then straighten. Repeat this short quick motion for sets of 20, and you'll feel the burn (and get toned arms too)! Remember, the straightened arm is not what we want to adopt in our regular stroke, but the strength we gain from this exercise is very beneficial.

**FIGURE 7.17** The tricep-only exercise on tubing builds strength in the upper arms that is very beneficial for swimmers.

Tubing is the perfect replacement workout if you cannot make it to a pool to swim. A 15-minute tubing workout can maintain the muscle tone you'll want when you get back in the water. It is easily packed in a suitcase and can be done in a hotel room, simply by attaching it to a door handle.

There are three levels of tension from which to choose, from light to heavy. Most athletes benefit most with the medium level. There is no risk of hurting yourself if you use a tension that is a bit more than you are ready to handle, but the primary focus should be on technique. Choose a level of resistance that allows you to hold proper technique.

You can do tubing every day, but even if you can only find time to do it 3 times per week, you will see tremendous gains in your swimming.

**Incorporate hand speed change.** Halo tubing is designed in length and tension to simulate the resistance an elite swimmer feels in the water throughout the pull path. Once you feel comfortable with the mechanics of the pull, take the next step by focusing on hand speed change throughout the pull back. Think of the finish as having a little "pop" or dynamic energy at the end. Remember that it is an acceleration action, so you do not have to muscle the tubing back.

## TRAINING WITH TUBING

To supplement your swim and strength training, aim to do tubing 3 times/week. Start with moderate sets, just as you would in the weight room when beginning a program. You can train in time increments (30 seconds, 45 seconds, or 1-minute repeats, for example) or by counting pulls (sets of 10, 20, 30, or 40 full pulls).

The following schedule and example sets are a guideline for training with tubing, and can be applied with or without a bench and template.

**Weeks 1–2:** Pull a light to moderate amount, and expect muscle soreness at first. Aim for 40–80 pulls per session, or 2–3 minutes of pulling time. For example, if you shoot for 60 pulls, you could divide the total up into 4 sets of 15, or 3 sets of 20, taking 1 minute or more rest between sets. If you aim for 3 minutes of pulling time, you can go 3 × 1:00, 4 × 0:45, or 6 × 0:30 with 1 minute or more rest between sets. Take the recovery you need between sets to execute the next set with good form.

**Weeks 3+:** Gradually increase the amount of tubing you do as you feel ready, ultimately building up to the following:

- Triathletes: 150–300 pulls or 5–7 minutes of pull time
- Swimmers (if not juggling other sports): 200–400 pulls or 6–10 minutes of pull time

## TUBING SET EXAMPLES

Here are three of my favorite go-to sets:

- To simulate my 200-meter freestyle race: 5 × 2 minutes at a 1.25 rate of turnover (this rate means I need to do 48 pulls per minute, so I watch a pace clock and count pulls—see Chapter 8 for details on how to calculate rate). Rest time between sets: 2 minutes.
- To build strength and feel the burn at the end: 6 × 1:30 as 1-minute full pulls and the last :30 triceps only (the burn!). Rest between sets: 1:30–2:00.
- To focus on form after making my triceps burn: 8 × 50 full pulls, as 20 triceps only (the burn!), then 30 full pulls (with great form).

Form goes hand in hand with strength and endurance in elite swimming. The drills and tubing exercises in this chapter help you develop both. For additional instruction, see a comprehensive set of videos at swimspeedsecrets.com. Most important of all, remember to have fun as you learn!

# 8

# PIECING IT ALL TOGETHER
## STROKE DATA & CONCLUSION

**WE'VE REACHED THE FINAL CHAPTER.** You've been drilled on mechanics, and done the bulk of the work necessary to understand this complex sport. There's a little bit more to learn, however, if we are to achieve the full effect we desire. We need to add the energetic and dynamic components to our vision of becoming efficient.

The goal of this chapter is to explain how to do that. We will revisit our swimming equation from Chapter 2 and piece everything together, showing the relevance of mechanics to that equation, as well as how rate of turnover comes into play.

Brew another coffee if you must. Do it to get through this chapter, or to celebrate that you are on the homestretch.

## STROKE COUNT AND DPS

Freestyle mechanics (and the drills and exercises designed to develop them) are the key to the "stroke count" side of our swimming equation. The mechanics—along with hand speed change—yield a generous return on investment called *distance per stroke.*

Distance per stroke (DPS) refers to the distance a body moves forward on each arm cycle. It is the truest way to determine the effectiveness of a swimmer's mechanics. I say "truest" because simply counting strokes is affected by variables such as the length of the pool and how long a swimmer stays underwater after pushing off the wall. To compare your stroke count with that of another swimmer, you must be in the same-length pool and surface to stroke at the same spot. DPS is a comparable number no matter the length of the pool or where a swimmer surfaces after diving in or pushing off the wall.

To better explain the relationship between stroke count and DPS, let's revisit Figure 2.1:

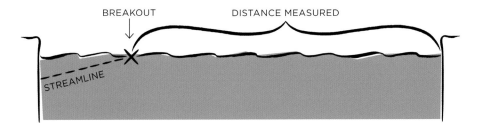

In the above illustration, you are in a 25-meter pool, and you streamline underwater to the 5-meter mark. Because you breakout at the 5-meter mark, you will be on the surface stroking for 20 meters. If you take 10 full strokes to cover the 20 meters, then you travel 2 meters per stroke (20 meters divided by 10 strokes). Your distance per stroke is 2 meters.

Figure 8.1 visually depicts the DPS concept by using the STGRID. Townley pulls with his right arm and travels forward three full grid squares from frame 1 to frame 8. Mastery of mechanics determines how far a swimmers' body moves forward.

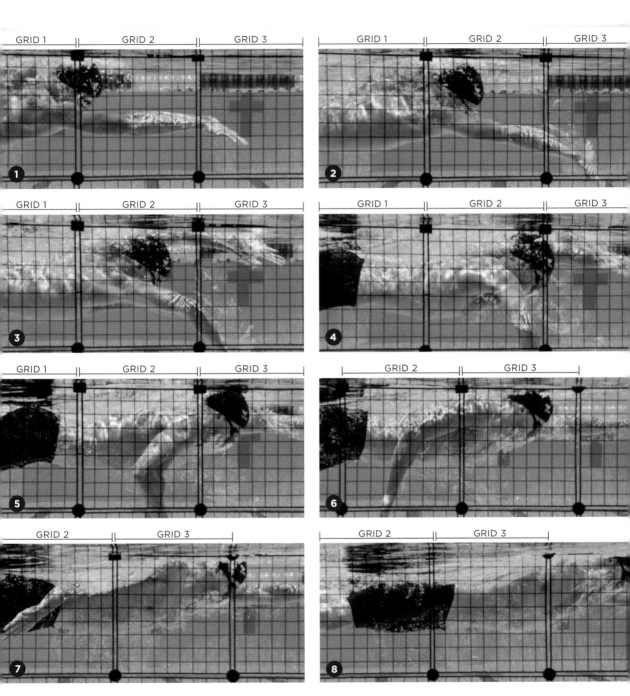

**FIGURE 8.1** DPS is the distance a swimmer's body moves forward on each stroke cycle. Note the distance Townley moves forward as he takes half a stroke cycle (right arm pulling).

You may choose to count strokes (10 in the above example) or calculate your DPS (2 meters per stroke in the above example). Either number tells you about the effectiveness of your stroking actions, and either number can be used to compare your stroking efficiency with other swimmers, as long as you know the details that ensure a relevant comparison.

The DPS calculation is handy because it can be transferred to pools of any length or any distance you swim. If, from our above example, you know that you travel 2 meters per stroke, then you can easily calculate how many strokes you should take in a 50-meter pool to achieve that same DPS.

For example, if you breakout at the 6-meter mark in a 50-meter pool, then you will be on the surface stroking for 44 meters. To achieve a DPS of 2 meters per stroke, you should complete the length in 22 stroke cycles. If you take more strokes—25, for example—then you know somewhere during that length your mechanics broke down due to fatigue or loss of focus. It is your job to regain the DPS through focus so you do not develop sloppy stroking habits.

In this chapter we will look at examples of stroke counts (and convert those to DPS) of elite swimmers in various freestyle races. We will also look at the other half of the equation: rate of turnover. From this complete set of numbers, we can establish goals for ourselves.

## RATE OF TURNOVER

Let's now get to the rate side of our efficiency goals and review how rate of turnover works. Rate is the time it takes you to complete a full stroke cycle. To calculate rate, use a stopwatch to time from the moment an arm enters the water until that same arm enters the water again in the same spot in the stroke cycle. That time is your rate for a full stroke cycle.

Rate varies greatly, depending on whether you are stroking easy or racing. *Generally speaking, a swimmer changes speed by changing rate.* Stroke

> ### FULL STROKE CYCLE
>
> When referring to stroke counts in this book, I refer to *full stroke cycles,* meaning a full revolution of both arms. Rather than counting every time an arm enters the water, I count from right arm entry until right arm entry again as 1 stroke (or left arm to left arm). Rate of turnover is timed for 1 full stroke cycle as well, from an arm entry until the same arm enters again.

count/DPS stays within a tight range on elite swimmers regardless of the rate of turnover they apply, but rate is more than twice as fast when a swimmer sprints versus goes easy. This is explained in further detail in upcoming sections, but first let's highlight the various rates of turnover seen in elite swimmers' strokes.

## THE GEAR SYSTEM

I developed a "gear" system for categorizing rate of turnover. There are approximately 7 gears in swimming, from easy recovery swimming to all-out sprint speed. The gears correlate with perceived effort as noted:

**Gear 1: Easy warm-up/warm-down/recovery swimming**
Rate of Turnover = 2.0–2.5 seconds per stroke cycle
Perceived effort < 60%

**Gear 2: Light aerobic, nonspecific swimming**
Rate of Turnover = 1.9–2.0 seconds per stroke cycle
Perceived effort = 60–70%

**Gear 3: Aerobic—base training**
Rate of Turnover = 1.7–1.8 seconds per stroke cycle
Perceived effort = 70–75%

### Gear 4: Endurance training
Rate of Turnover = 1.5–1.6 seconds per stroke cycle
Perceived effort = 75–83%

### Gear 5: Mid-distance and distance race tempo (200-meter free and longer)
Rate of Turnover = 1.25–1.5 seconds per stroke cycle
Perceived effort = 83–90%

### Gear 6: 100-meter race tempo
Rate of Turnover = 1.0–1.30 seconds per stroke cycle
Perceived effort = 90–95%

### Gear 7: All-out sprint; 50-meter race tempo
Rate of Turnover = 0.85–1.0 seconds per stroke cycle
Perceived effort = 100%

---

### CONVERTING RATE TO CYCLES PER MINUTE

Just as stroke count can be converted to DPS, rate of turnover can be converted to stroke cycles per minute. Some books and articles use stroke cycles per minute to describe rate, and while I do not use that method in this book, I want you to understand how to make the simple conversion.

If a swimmer completes a full stroke cycle in 1.0 second, then that swimmer's rate can be stated as 60 cycles per minute, calculated as:

$$\frac{60 \text{ seconds}}{1 \text{ second per stroke}}$$

If a swimmer takes 2.0 seconds to complete a stroke cycle, then their rate is 30 cycles/minute (60 seconds divided by 2 seconds/stroke). Some charts list various rates of turnover, such as 48 cycles per minute, 42, 51, 64, etc. To convert stroke cycles per minute to the rates I include in this book, divide the number into 60. So a rate of 64 cycles per minute is converted as: 60/64 = 0.94 seconds per stroke.

Gears 1–3 are primarily training gears. Gears 5–7 are racing gears (which you must do in training as well, to prepare for your races). Gear 4 can be either, depending on the distance as well as a swimmer's fitness and conditioning.

You should know how to choose the appropriate gear(s) for your training set or race. Moreover, you must be patient over weeks and months of your season to build fitness and coordination to apply the faster gears effectively—that is, to maintain effective mechanics as you pick up your rate.

Achieving desired rates of turnover is not a simple task, because a swimmer must maintain DPS while striving for faster rates. For instance, if you note that a 100-meter freestyler at the Olympics strokes at a rate of 1.10 and you get excited to hit that rate but spin your wheels and add strokes to do so, then you're sacrificing one half of the swimming equation (stroke count) for the other half (rate).

DPS is your foundation. A mature mindset in swimming is always attuned to DPS, and rate adjusts accordingly. Propulsive pull mechanics, hand speed change, kick mechanics, kick timing, and other freestyle components described in this book are present in elite strokes even when they're racing in gears 5, 6, and 7.

Because the underwater pull is the vital element of the stroke, DPS is effectively achieved only if a swimmer is adept at the propulsive phases of the stroke. DPS is not effectively achieved from actions such as gliding. Gliding (holding the hand/arm extended in front of the shoulder during the nonpropulsive extension phase of the stroke) is a buzz-kill for the rate of turnover side of our equation.

The underwater pull path, from the catch to the finish, establishes a swimmer's baseline DPS (kicking—the other propulsive part of the stroke—also contributes). The nonvital elements of the stroke affect DPS as well. To clarify, though, these nonvital elements do not establish DPS; rather, they *affect* it. For instance, a swimmer does not benefit if the hand/arm entering the water chops in wide of shoulder width and additional surface area of the arm is exposed to the water's resistance, negatively impacting the baseline DPS you achieved from the propulsive stroking (and kicking) actions. Neither does poor body position or nonoptimal stroke timing help your cause. But none of these nonvital elements move you forward in the water. The only part of the stroke that does that, and hence gives you your starting point for DPS, is the propulsive pull (and kick). All other factors can take away from that, but the propulsive parts of the stroke set the baseline.

I encourage athletes to first focus on feeling the distance their body moves during the propulsive phases of the stroke, and then attend to the additional parts of the stroke that impact the baseline DPS, ensuring they allow you to get the most from your propulsive stroking action.

## TRAINING MATTERS

There are no shortcuts. The combination of DPS and rate requires attention to detail, toughness, and dynamism.

The condition you're in matters; therefore, training matters.

When I was pursuing triathlon full-time, I trained to swim the first 200–300 meters of a race in gear 5 (1.3 rate of turnover) in order to break away from the field. Maintaining that rate for the entire 1,500-meter swim would not have been a wise use of energy considering a 40K bike and 10K run followed, so once I broke away I settled into gear 4 (approximately 1.5 rate). If I tried that strategy today, with no training, I would last for approximately 10 seconds in gear 5, and then I would have to shut it down to gear 2 (maybe gear 1) just to survive the rest of the 1,500-meter swim. *Rate must be trained.* I had to get in condition in order to execute my race strategy when I was seriously training for triathlon.

If you do not have time or do not make sport a high priority, then realistic adjustments must be made to your rate expectations. Your stroke count (DPS) should not change due to minimal training, but you will need to shift rate to easier gears.

A classic example of this is seen in 1984 Olympic gold medalist Rowdy Gaines's data comparison between 1980 (at the height of his career, training full-time) and 2011 (as a masters swimmer in the 50–54-year-old age group, training minimally a few days a week).

Data collected from two of Rowdy's 200-meter freestyle races shows his stroke count/DPS did not change between 1980 and 2011. At the 1980 race,

Rowdy finished the 200-meter freestyle in 1:50.02 and took 81 full stroke cycles over the course of the race. Thirty-one years later, in 2011, as a masters swimmer, Rowdy finished the 200-meter freestyle in 2:03.51, and his over-all stroke count for the 200 meters was 80. Rowdy took 1 full stroke less as a masters swimmer training minimally. *His DPS did not change* (it actually was a little better in 2011). The comparison is relevant, because both races were in a 50-meter pool, and Rowdy surfaced at the same spot—between the 4–5 meter mark—in each race.

What did change between 1980 and 2011 was Rowdy's rate of turnover. Rate accounted for that 13.5-second difference in time. In 1980 Rowdy's rate was 1.25 seconds per stroke cycle for the first 150 meters of the race, and he came home in 1.15 on the last 50. In 2011 he swam the first 50 meters with a 1.35–1.40 rate before settling into a 1.40–1.45 rate for the remaining 150 meters. On average, his rate in 2011 was 0.15 slower than in 1980 throughout the race. Although 0.15 may seem insignificant, it adds up over the course of 80 stroke cycles.

**80 strokes × 0.15 seconds/stroke = 12 seconds**

The actual difference in time was 13.5 seconds, but the 12 seconds in the calculation above is near-enough to confirm what the data shows—that rate is the culprit for the slower time, not DPS.

Rowdy's example drives home the point that DPS is not affected by age or training, but rate is affected by both of those factors.

Every swimmer, whether young and in the prime of their career or older and just trying to squeeze in a practice when time and energy permit, can count on DPS being tried and true once it's developed and seared into your stroke. Once DPS is solidly established via stroke mechanics, stroke rate is what to work on next. *And rate must be trained!*

If a coach gives a set of 8 × 50 at max effort, with 2 minutes rest between repeats (plenty of rest), to a group of high school swimmers, and some of those athletes are turning over at a 1.3 rate of turnover, the coach can immediately stop the set and use rate as a teaching moment for what "max" effort entails—a 1.0 or faster rate for that age group. Of course, the coach must also remind the swimmers to keep their focus on DPS. Some swimmers may spin their wheels, slipping their arms through the water rather than accelerating water back, unknowingly increasing their stroke count as they try to attain the 1.0 rate. It takes discipline, toughness, and focus to keep awareness on DPS while ratcheting up rate to the higher gears.

Rate of turnover expectations for older swimmers are different. For masters swimmers in their 40s and 50s, I add approximately 0.2 to the rates we see in elite swimmers' strokes. So, if a 50-year old is doing the same set as above (8 × 50 at max effort with 2 minutes rest between), then the goal rate is 1.2 rather than 1.0. For those age 60 and over, and depending on an athlete's general strength and condition, rate can be adjusted appropriately. A 75-year-old female masters swimmer may have a top-end sprint rate of 1.8, which is perfectly fine. The goal is to set specific rate goals for each swimmer and impart on them that sprint rates should always be faster than easy aerobic swimming rates—and, of course, that DPS must be maintained in all gears.

**DPS = technique**

**Rate = fitness**

## WHEN IS ADDING A STROKE OK?

We know we need to maintain DPS as we change gears in swimming. But we're human. Fatigue sets in, even for Olympians. Stroke counts/DPS change to a degree throughout a race. In distance races, such as the 800-meter freestyle and longer, DPS is very consistent because swimmers hold back from maximal output at the start of the race. Thus, longer races are much more evenly paced. But in races such as the 100-meter and 200-meter freestyle, swimmers walk a fine line of high output during the first half of the race and experience lactic acid burn in the muscles during the latter part of the race. It's a suffer-fest. In these cases, stroke counts go up (DPS goes down) slightly as the race progresses. It is not uncommon to see elite swimmers add $\frac{1}{2}$, 1, or sometimes $1\frac{1}{2}$ stroke cycles per 50 meters as they near the end of such a race.

The increase in stroke count should be due to physical fatigue, however, not mechanical breakdown due to loss of focus.

You have control over this in training. A good rule of thumb when you train is to check your stroke count occasionally, especially during endurance and high-quality sets that cause fatigue, and if your stroke count creeps to 2 stroke cycles or more per 50 meters than your normal count during lighter aerobic training, there is a mechanical breakdown somewhere in your stroke as you try to go faster. Regain your focus and get your DPS where it needs to be. If you do so, this moment of fatigue is when you make the most strides in becoming a stronger, better swimmer.

Sprinting is another area that increases stroke count (decreases DPS). Elite sprinters are willing to sacrifice DPS slightly in order to achieve fast rates of turnover, but only to a point. DPS is still their bread and butter. Once again, we can set a general rule of thumb for this for individual swimmers: If, for example, you take 8 full stroke cycles to complete a length of the pool swimming in gear 2–3, then when sprinting, it is OK to add 1 full stroke cycle, and even 1.5, per 25 meters (2–3 stroke cycles per 50 meters). But if your stroke count creeps up 2 full stroke cycles per 25 (4 per 50), then your mechanics are breaking down somewhere. You're spinning your wheels, tending more to the rate side of the equation and losing focus on DPS.

## SETTING DATA GOALS

What is a respectable DPS? How many strokes per 25 yards or meters does an elite swimmer take, and how many should you set as a goal? These numbers vary from swimmer to swimmer, but we can look at actual elite data examples and then do some basic calculations to give you an idea of what is required to achieve goal times you may have for yourself.

Let's look at two examples of elite swimmers' data.

We'll start with Katie Ledecky's gold medal and world record swim in the 800-meter freestyle from the 2016 Olympics. Because the 800 is a distance event, Ledecky's data was quite consistent throughout the race.

She surfaced at the 6-meter mark off the turns, which means Ledecky was on the surface stroking for 44 meters (the Olympics are contested in a 50-meter pool).

She took 20.5 stroke cycles on the majority of the lengths, which is a DPS of 2.15 meters per stroke (44 meters on the surface swimming, divided by 20.5 stroke cycles).

Her rate of turnover was in the 1.32 seconds per stroke cycle range.

Let's do the math:

$$20.5 \text{ strokes} \times 1.32 \text{ seconds/stroke} = 27.06 \text{ seconds}$$

Ledecky is on the surface stroking for 27.06 seconds every 50 meters.

There are two other factors we need to add to the 27.06 seconds to get her full 50-meter split on each length:

- The amount of time she is underwater streamlining off the turns to the 6-meter mark.
- How long it takes her to make the turn, from her last hand entry before the wall, until she somersaults and plants her feet on the wall to push off.

Ledecky spends 2.25 seconds underwater streamlining to the 6-meter mark, and 1.0 second to make the turn. Let's plug in these numbers and add them to the 27.06 seconds that she is on the surface stroking:

$$2.25 + 1.0 = 3.25 \text{ seconds}$$
$$3.25 + 27.06 = 30.31 \text{ seconds}$$

The 30.31 seconds is approximately the time she takes on each 50 meters.

There are 16 lengths in the 800-meter freestyle in a 50-meter pool, and we see the data matches up quite accurately with her gold-medal, world-record time of 8:04.79 from those Olympic Games:

**16 lengths of the pool × 30.31 = 8:04.96**

From this data, swimmers can target aspects of Ledecky's swim—whether it be rate, DPS/stroke count, or turn data. Sometimes a swimmer seems unbeatable, but the data behind that swimmer's performance is another story. The data is measureable and doable. The question is whether swimmers have the gumption to train with focus and toughness to achieve the data.

For our second example, let's look at the data of a male sprinter. Here are the details behind Nathan Adrian's 100-meter freestyle gold-medal swim at the 2012 Olympics.

- **Time:** 47.52
- **First 50:** Adrian surfaced at the 11-meter mark off the start (he was underwater for 3.4 seconds) and took 16.5 strokes. His DPS was 2.36 meters per stroke (39 meters divided by 16.5 strokes), and rate of turnover was 1.15–1.20.
- **Second 50:** Adrian surfaced at the 7-meter mark off the turn (underwater for 2.5 seconds) and took 19 strokes at a rate of 1.15–1.20. His DPS on this 50 was 2.26 meters per stroke (43 meters divided by 19 strokes).

The examples of Ledecky and Adrian give us the gist of how to calculate DPS and other data. The Appendix includes additional data calculations and analysis, but for those who just want the quick-hit numbers, Figure 8.2 outlines stroke counts, DPS, and rate. These numbers are an average from the middle lengths of the race. From this, we start to see ranges in the data and can use those to formulate goals for ourselves.

| ATHLETE AND EVENT | Olympic Year | Time | Stroke Count | Rate | Surfaced at (m) | DPS (m/stroke) |
|---|---|---|---|---|---|---|
| Katie Ledecky 800 free | 2016 | 8:04.79 | 20.5 | 1.32 | 6 | 2.15 |
| Rebecca Adlington 800 free | 2008 | 8:14.10 | 20.0 | 1.38–1.40 | 5 | 2.25 |
| Allison Schmitt 200 free | 2012 | 1:53.61 | 19.0 | 1.35 | 7 | 2.26 |
| Peter Vanderkaay 200 free (in 800 free relay) | 2008 | 1:44.68 (split) | 16.5 | 1.4 | 8 | 2.54 |
| Park Tae-Hwan 400 free | 2008 | 3:41.86 | 17.0 | 1.5 | 6 | 2.58 |
| Park Tae-Hwan 200 free | 2008 | 1:44.85 (silver medal) | 18.0 | 1.35 | 6 | 2.44 |
| Simone Manuel 100 free | 2016 | 52.70 | 19.0 | 1.30 | 8 | 2.21 |
| Nathan Adrian 100 free | 2012 | 47.52 | 19.0 | 1.15–1.20 | 7 | 2.26 |
| Alain Bernard 100 free | 2008 | 47.21 | 20.0 | 1.1 | 7 | 2.17 |

Notes: Peter surfaced at the 8-meter mark in 2.8 seconds. Simone surfaced at the 8-meter mark off the turn in 3.2 seconds.

FIGURE 8.2 Olympic swimmers' freestyle performances in a 50-meter pool.

The swimmers listed in Figure 8.2 (except Simone Manuel and Peter Vanderkaay) surfaced between the 5–7-meter mark off the turn. They were underwater for 2.0–2.5 seconds. These are gold-medal winning Olympic swims in a 50-meter pool (Park Tae-Hwan's 200-free is a silver-medal swim but is included alongside his gold-medal 400-free data for comparison).

Notice that all of the Olympic freestylers range from 2.15 to 2.58 meters per stroke for DPS, with the women ranging in the lower end at 2.15–2.26, and the men generally higher, 2.17–2.58. Other than a couple of examples (Park Tae-Hwan and Peter Vanderkaay), a stroke count of 19–20 in a 50-meter pool is quite common among Olympic swimmers.

| ATHLETE AND EVENT | Competition | Time | Stroke Count | Rate | Surfaced at (yd.) | DPS (yd./stroke) (m/stroke) |
|---|---|---|---|---|---|---|
| Missy Franklin 200 free split on 800 free relay | 2014 NCAAs | 1:40.08 | 8.0 | 1.30 | 6 | 2.37 2.17 |
| Chase Kalisz 100 free split at end of 400 IM | 2014 NCAAs | 50.93 | 7.5 | 1.35 | 5 | 2.67 2.44 |
| Townley Haas 200 free | 2016 NCAAs | 1:30.46 | 7.0 | 1.25 | 7 | 2.57 2.35 |
| Rowdy Gaines 100 free | 2010 Masters Championships* | 46.90 | 7.5–8.0 | 1.25 | 5 | 2.5–2.66 2.28–2.43 |
| Vladimir Morozov 100 free | 2013 NCAAs | 40.76 | 7.5 | 1.00 | 8 | 2.26 2.06 |
| Vladimir Morozov 50 free relay split on 200 free relay | 2013 NCAAs | 17.86 (split) | 9.0 | 0.85–0.90 | 7 | 2.0 1.82 |

* 50–54 age group.

FIGURE 8.3 Olympic swimmers' freestyle performances in a 25-yard pool.

Figure 8.3 shows examples of freestyle swims in a 25-yard pool. The Olympic swimmers in these examples surfaced between the 5–7-yard mark off the turn (other than Vladimir Morozov in the 100 free, who surfaced at the 8-yard mark) and were underwater for 2.0 seconds on average.

Here, we have converted DPS in yards per stroke to meters per stroke so we can compare to the examples in Figure 8.2, which are from a 50-meter pool. To make the conversion, multiply the DPS in yards per stroke by 0.9144 because 1 yard = 0.9144 meter.)

Once again, we see the DPS fall into the same range as in the examples from a 50-meter pool, with the exception being Vladimir Morozov in the 50- and 100-free. He is willing to give up some DPS to achieve extremely high rates of turnover.

We also see that elite freestylers in a 25-yard pool generally take 7–8 full stroke cycles if they surface between the 5–7 yard mark (other than Vladimir's 9 stroke count in the 50-free relay split).

## CALCULATING YOUR GOAL TIMES

What should you shoot for? If you're in the prime of your swim career with lofty goals, then target the elite data. On the other hand, some swimmers are happy with improvements over time, simply for the intrinsic reward of seeing progress, or to narrow the gap in a triathlon so they don't have to make up as much time on the bike and run.

Using the same formula we've been studying, let's look at how you can plug in numbers to map out your personal goal times.

From previous examples of elite swimmers we know the data is broken down into four major segments: stroke count, rate of turnover, time spent underwater off the wall, and time to make the turn.

The time spent underwater and the time it takes to make the turn are numbers that are mostly fixed. On average, an elite swimmer stays underwater in a streamline position off the turns for 2.0–2.5 seconds before surfacing to stroke. The head breaks the surface at approximately the 5–7-meter mark on average.

When I work with swimmers at my clinics, I use a fixed number of 2.5 seconds for their streamline underwater.

The other relatively fixed number in elite data is the time to make the turn. On average, top swimmers make the turn in 1.0 second. At clinics, I give swimmers a fixed number of 1.5 seconds to make the turn, whether they do a flip turn or an open hand touch turn.

The two fixed numbers in our goal calculations, therefore, are 2.5 seconds underwater off the turns, and 1.5 seconds to make the turn, which equals 4.0 seconds we will add to every length of the pool, whether in a 25-yard, 25-meter, or

---

Note: Time and distance underwater off the start is slightly longer than off the turns. Elite swimmers are underwater on average for 3–4 seconds and travel 9–11 meters before surfacing to stroke off the start. We will only use turn data in the upcoming examples).

---

50-meter pool (note: if you want to target elite data, then set a fixed number of 3.5 seconds for this, which accounts for 1.0 to make the turn, and 2.5 underwater).

Now, we'll take a goal time that is fairly common among triathletes and adult swimmers—1:30 per 100 yards—and work backwards to determine realistic stroke count and rate data. You can choose any goal time and do the following calculations.

**Step 1. Calculate the time per length.** In our example, we want to achieve 1:30 for a 100-yard freestyle. Since we're in a 25-yard pool, divide 1:30 by 4 lengths of the pool. This equals 22.5 seconds per 25-yard length.

**Step 2. Calculate the time spent swimming on the surface.** We have established a fixed number of 4 seconds to make the turn and streamline underwater, so subtract 4 seconds from the 22.5 seconds we do for each 25 yards. 22.5 seconds minus 4 seconds = 18.5 seconds.

- The 18.5 seconds is the amount of time we are on the surface stroking. And the 18.5 seconds will be composed of stroke count and stroke rate.

**Step 3. Determine your stroke count.** When you swim, count your strokes. Keep in mind that the examples in this book are of *full stroke cycles,* so the method for counting is as follows:

- **Push off the wall and streamline underwater.** When your first arm breaks the surface and recovers overwater and then the hand on that arm enters the water, count stroke count #1. Every time that same hand enters the water, count the next stroke. So, if your right arm is the first to break the surface and hit the water, then count a stroke every time the right arm enters the water.

**Step 4. Determine the rate you need to hit.** To do so, take the number determined in Step 2 (the time spent on the surface stroking), and divide it by the number of strokes taken. Let's say you have a stroke count of 10 full strokes per 25 yards. In Step 2 we determined that we are on the surface stroking for 18.5 seconds to reach our goal time of 1:30 for the 100:

$$\frac{18.5 \text{ seconds}}{10 \text{ strokes}} = 1.85 \text{ seconds/stroke}$$

To achieve a time of 1:30 per 100, with a stroke count of 10, requires that a swimmer stroke at 1.85 seconds per stroke cycle.

This example assumes that a swimmer is pushing off the wall on every length rather than doing a start off the starting blocks. This is accurate for pacing a distance event or generally targeting data you want to hit in the middle of a race such as a 200 free. If you really want to dig into your data for a race such as a 50 or 100 free (and the full 200 free), study the examples in the Appendix, which go into detail analyzing elite performances.

## IS 10 STROKES A REALISTIC NUMBER?

If a swimmer surfaces at the 5-yard mark and takes 10 strokes to complete the 25-yard length of the pool, then his/her DPS is 2 yards per stroke (20 yards divided by 10 strokes). A DPS of 2 yards per stroke is doable and respectable. You can achieve some great times with a stroke count of 10. When I coach triathletes and adult swimmers for whom swimming is not their top priority—and some young swimmers—I set 10 full strokes per 25 yards as a basic standard. As they work on mechanics, then, getting the count down to 9.5, 9, and lower is even better, as long as they achieve the better counts as a result of efficiency on the propulsive stroking components and other stroke elements from Chapter 6, *not from gliding*!

We've seen that elite swimmers get those counts down to 7–8 strokes (surfacing between the 5–7-yard mark), achieving a DPS of 2.3–2.6 yards per stroke. Their mechanics are quite solid to achieve these numbers. Counts less than 7 strokes per 25 yards will be seen in elite swimmers, but those athletes are either surfacing past the 7-yard mark (such as off the start, or longer time spent

## HOW TO CALCULATE YOUR STROKE RATE

To get your rate of turnover, you have two options:

**Use a stopwatch.** Have someone use a stopwatch to time how long it takes you to do a full stroke cycle. He or she will time from the moment one hand hits the water on entry until that same hand enters again in the same spot in the stroke cycle. The time that takes equals your rate. Take the rate multiple times to get an idea of the average number. You can also time two full stroke cycles and then divide by 2 to get your rate. This reduces some of the natural human error when trying to start the watch at the exact moment of entry.

**Use a tempo trainer.** Wear a waterproof trainer, which fits around the ear or in the swim cap, set to a desired rate. The trainer beeps at the set rate as the swimmer synchs the arms to hit in timing with the beeping.

dolphin kicking underwater off the turns) or are stroking with slightly slower rates of turnover, such as 1.4–1.6 seconds per stroke cycle.

Ultimately you plug in numbers you believe are attainable, but as a starting point, 2 yards per stroke DPS (equal to 1.8 meters per stroke—which is a stroke count of 11 in a 25-meter pool assuming the swimmer surfaces at the 5-meter mark) is doable for any swimmer who concentrates on mechanics.

Don't worry if you can't hit the DPS of 2 yards per stroke (1.8 meters/stroke) yet. Many athletes I see at clinics have counts of 12–14 strokes in a 25-yard pool. That is OK. Their mechanics and/or hand speed change is not dialed in yet. Attention to the mechanics detailed in this book is the key to improving DPS/stroke count. Be patient and chip away at it. Always remember, though, that effectively achieving solid stroke count numbers requires attending to propulsive stroking actions, not gliding.

## GUIDELINES AND REMINDERS

You now have enough information to set goals for yourself by plugging in numbers. To do so effectively, here are a few guidelines and reminders:

## THE EFFECT OF RATE—IT ADDS UP!

Keeping our stroke count at 10, let's study the effect various rates of turnover have on our time. We will use the 100-yard freestyle as our event. Following are examples of 10 strokes at rates of turnover that are just 0.5 different—a seemingly not significant difference:

**Example 1: Rate of Turnover 1.7**

10 strokes × 1.7 rate of turnover = 17 seconds on the surface stroking

17 seconds + 4 seconds to make turn and streamline underwater
= 21 seconds per 25 yards

This equates to 42 seconds per 50, and a 1:24 for the 100.

**Example 2: Rate of Turnover 1.2**

10 strokes × 1.2 rate of turnover = 12 seconds on the surface stroking

12 seconds + 4 seconds to make turn and streamline underwater
= 16 seconds per 25 yards

This equates to 32 seconds per 50, and a 1:04 for the 100.

As you can see, a rate difference of 0.5 per stroke equates to a 20-second difference in time for 100 yards, with a stroke count of 10 per 25 yards.

This is an extreme example, in which the 0.5 seconds in rate difference accumulates throughout the entire swim, but rate also adds up in bits and pieces during a race, and it oftentimes leaves swimmers getting touched out by another swimmer at the finish or missing a cutoff time by tenths or hundredths of a second. The most common example occurs when swimmers slow their rate going into a turn. Swimmers who lose focus or lack aggressiveness going into the turn slow their rate by 0.2–0.5 seconds per stroke on the last 2–3 stroke cycles into each wall. Even slowing by 0.2 for two stroke cycles adds 0.4 to that turn. If there are three turns in a 100-yard race, then a swimmer can end up with a time 1.2 seconds slower. Focus into the walls and keep your rate.

Rate adds up!

- **In a 25-yard pool, Olympic medalists take 7–8 strokes per length when they surface around the 5–7-yard mark.** As a starting point, 10 strokes is very respectable, so when calculating your goals, plug in stroke count numbers between 7 and 10, depending on what you feel is doable. (Add 1 to these stroke counts when in a 25-meter pool, as a meter is approximately 10 percent longer than a yard.)

- **Learn the mechanics at slow rates.** Most of the drills in this book are best done slowly, without concern for rate of turnover. As you feel more confident in your DPS at slower rates, try applying faster rates of turnover to the stroke and see if you can maintain stroke count/DPS.

- **All rates of turnover, whether slow or race-pace fast, require that hand speed changes.** When you practice faster rates of turnover, you will make the catch faster than when swimming easy, but make sure that you increase hand speed through the finish. And when you drill or swim slowly, don't hold slow hand speed throughout the propulsive phases. End the stroke with a light dynamic, accelerated touch.

- **Rates of turnover among elite swimmers are typically 0.05–0.1 faster in a 25-yard or 25-meter pool than they are in a 50-meter pool.** This is due to the power from pushing off the wall. So, when calculating your goal data for a race in a 25-yard or 25-meter pool, consider plugging in rate of turnover data that is slightly faster than what you plug in for the same race in a 50-meter pool.

- **Practice rate of turnover out of the water to maintain mechanics and rate in the water.** You can simulate your actual race tempo with tubing training (see Chapter 7). For example, I targeted a 1.25 rate of turnover for my 200-meter freestyle race. A 1.25 rate equates to 48 full pull cycles per minute, so when I trained with tubing, I ensured 48 pulls per minute for 2-minute repeats. I did 5 × 2 minute repeats at this rate, with 2 minutes rest between sets.

## CONCLUSION

It's not hard to see why elite swimmers are breaking records left and right. They are optimizing the equation from Chapter 2, taking fewer strokes at a faster rate and accomplishing it via technically astute propulsive stroking.

Elite swimmers are by nature hard workers, but their work is only meaningful because of their mechanics. The masses of swimmers and triathletes who train diligently day after day and see no improvement in their times are not making progress because they have nothing solid upon which to place the hard work. Happily, we can change that.

You may not have a six-figure sponsorship or access to the top training equipment that some elites have, but you have access to the same water. Water does not discriminate. It is ours for the taking. So, do what Johnny Weissmuller did, and get a purchase on the elusive.

This is your life! You may get euchred if you take a risk, but at least you boldly played the game. In cards, "getting euchred" means that you called the trump suit but your competition was dealt a better hand and beat you. It happens occasionally in life, too. I got euchred during the fencing portion of the pentathlon in Beijing. It was still worth it!

Call the suit!

# APPENDIX:
## STROKE DATA ANALYSIS

For those interested in stroke data, this appendix presents five case studies intended to give swimmers deeper insights into freestyle performances. To fully understand the information here, be sure to first read Chapter 8 on stroke data. The five case studies are:

- **A comparison of what it takes to go 1:30 versus 1:40 in the 200-yard free.** We will look at the data of Townley Haas (1:30.46) and Missy Franklin (1:40.08 relay split) side by side, and see that seemingly insignificant differences in data add up over the course of a race.

- **The most amazing example of maintaining DPS I've ever seen.** Simone Manuel, 2016 Olympic champion in the 100 m free, maintained her distance per stroke for the duration of the race more impressively than any athlete I've ever studied. We can be inspired and challenged to approach her mental and physical toughness.

- **What it means to "work the 3rd 50 of a 200."** Whereas most swimmers fall off pace midway through a 200 m race, learn how Olympic gold medalist Peter Vanderkaay keeps his pace after the midway point.

- **Hope for short swimmers.** Is being shorter necessarily a disadvantage when racing a taller swimmer? Stroke data does not care about your height. In this mini-study, I show my own data as a 5′ 2 ½″ swimmer.

- **A 100 m freestyle comparison: Mark Spitz 1972 data and Nathan Adrian 2012 data.** For the math aficionados, this case study is my infatuation with the sport at its finest.

## A COMPARISON OF WHAT IT TAKES TO GO 1:30 VERSUS 1:40 IN THE 200-YARD FREE

A 10-second difference in finish time for a race is notable, but when looking at the data behind the time, you might be surprised how slight differences add up.

| | MISSY FRANKLIN | TOWNLEY HAAS |
|---|---|---|
| **EVENT** | 2014 NCAA Championships 200-Yard Freestyle Relay Split | 2016 NCAA Championships 200-Yard Freestyle Individual Event |
| **Time** | 1:40.08 | 1:30.46 |
| **Stroke Count Average per 25** | 8 | 7 |
| **DPS** | 2.37 yards/stroke (2.17 meters/stroke) | 2.57 yards/stroke (2.35 meters/stroke) |
| **Average Turnover Rate** | 1.25 seconds per stroke | 1.22–1.30 seconds per stroke |
| **Turn Data** | Surfaced at the 6-yard mark off the turns in 2.2 seconds | Surfaced at the 7-yard mark off the turns in 2.2 seconds |

Missy and Townley stroke with the same rate of turnover average—1.25 seconds per stroke. They spend the same amount of time underwater off the turns (2.2 seconds). It is the difference in stroke count—Missy's 8 and Townley's 7—that accounts for the 10-second difference. Missy takes 1 more stroke than Townley each 25 yards. There are 8 lengths in the 200-yard freestyle, which means she takes 8 strokes more over the course of the race. If we multiply

8 strokes by 1.25 seconds per stroke (rate), we get the 10-second difference in overall finish time.

## THE MOST AMAZING EXAMPLE OF MAINTAINING DPS I'VE EVER SEEN

The 2016 women's Olympic 100 m freestyle champion, Simone Manuel (USA), swam a race the likes of which I've never seen. She tied for gold with Penny Oleksiak (Canada) with a time of 52.70, but it is Simone's data that takes swimming to new heights:

**SIMONE MANUEL**

Time: 52.70

| 100 m FREESTYLE | 1st 50 | 2nd 50 |
|---|---|---|
| Number of Strokes | 17.5 | 19 |
| DPS (meters/stroke) | 2.28 | 2.21 |
| Average Turnover Rate | 1.20–1.30 seconds per stroke | 1.20–1.30 seconds per stroke |
| Start and Turn Data | Surfaced in 4.1 seconds at the 10 m mark off the start | Surfaced in 3.2 seconds to the 8 m mark off the turn |

This is an incredible example of maintaining DPS at a 100 m freestyle rate of turnover. Simone's DPS barely suffered on the second 50. She went from 2.28 meters per stroke on the first 50 to 2.21 on the second 50. The training and maturity to achieve this takes swimming to new heights. At practice, check your stroke count occasionally as you're in the thick of a tough set, and train to maintain DPS.

As a side note, the time it took Simone to make the turn in this Olympic race was 0.8 seconds—the quickest I've ever seen. Do you work your turns in practice? I think Simone does.

## WHAT IT MEANS TO "WORK THE 3RD 50 OF A 200"

One purpose of this book is to define traditionally vague swimming concepts with measureable parameters. In this data example, I explain a popular race strategy concept: "work the 3rd 50 of your 200!"

Many swimmers have heard these words from a coach, yet it remains a vague command that translates to: "This is going to hurt." Yes, discomfort begins to set in at this point in a 200, but there is more to understand. We can specifically define "work the 3rd 50" with numbers, by studying the data behind Olympic 200 m performances. In this example we look at Peter Vanderkaay's 200 m freestyle split on the 800 m freestyle relay at the 2008 Olympics in Beijing.

### PETER VANDERKAAY

Time: 1:44.68

| 200 m FREESTYLE | 1st 50 | 2nd 50 | 3rd 50 | 4th 50 |
|---|---|---|---|---|
| **Number of Strokes** | 14 | 15 | 16.5 | 17.5 |
| **DPS (meters/stroke)** | 2.78 | 2.8 | 2.54 | 2.4 |
| **Average Turnover Rate** | 1.55 | 1.55 | 1.40 | 1.37 |
| **Start and Turn Data** | Surfaced at the 11 m mark off the start in 3.6 seconds | Surfaced at the 8 m mark in 2.8 seconds off the turn | Surfaced at 8 m mark off the turn | Surfaced at 8 m mark off the turn |

Peter starts the race with a 2.78 DPS, and midway through, on the 3rd 50, shortens to a 2.54 DPS. This is normal due to fatigue. Notice, however, that he picks up his rate of turnover on the 3rd 50 to a 1.40 from the 1.55 rate at the beginning of the race. The increased rate of turnover is purposely applied to make up for the loss of DPS.

When a coach tells a swimmer to "work the 3rd 50 of a 200," it means to work your rate of turnover. Rate naturally slows at this point in the race due to fatigue, just as DPS does, but with proper training, tough swimmers can pick up their rate to make up for the natural slight loss of DPS. You must still concentrate on maintaining DPS as best you can. When you pick up rate, do not spin your wheels.

Let's look at the effect "working the 3rd 50" has on split times between the 2nd and 3rd 50s of Peter's 200. To calculate the times we have to multiply the stroke count and rates from the 2nd and 3rd 50s:

> 2nd 50: 15.0 strokes × 1.55 seconds/stroke = 23.25 seconds
> 3rd 50: 16.5 strokes × 1.40 seconds/stroke = 23.10 seconds

You can see that even though Peter added 1.5 strokes on the 3rd 50, he maintained his pace (23.25 to 23.10) by picking up his rate.

The above splits are Peter's time spent stroking on the surface only. To get the actual split times on the 50s above, we need to add the time spent to make the turn, plus the time spent underwater off the turn. Those are the same for each 50 (approximately 2.8 underwater off the turn and 1.1 to make the turn). It is the shift in stroke count and rate that are important in this example.

Oh, by the way, on the last 50 Peter picks up his rate even more (to 1.37), to make up for the shortening DPS. This is an Olympic champion's strategy. It can be yours too, if you train for it!

## HOPE FOR SHORT SWIMMERS

Occasionally I receive emails from parents of shorter swimmers wanting advice for their child about how to have confidence racing taller swimmers. I'm just shy of 5'3" and never felt "short" when I was in the water racing. Why? Because I could feel the DPS I got on each stroke.

Following is my data from some practice swims in the last few years.

When I swim a light aerobic set, I take 8 strokes per 25 yards, surfacing at the 6-yard mark. My DPS is 2.37 yards/stroke (2.17 meters/stroke).

When I push off a 100-yard freestyle in practice at max effort, my stroke count goes up to 9 and rate is 1.15 (if I'm in shape). I don't have a powerful dolphin kick underwater so I spend only 2.0 seconds underwater—to the 5-yard mark. My DPS in this scenario is 2.2 yards/stroke (2.03 meters/stroke).

The data adds up as follows:

**9 strokes × 1.15 rate = 10.35 seconds on the surface stroking**

I take 1.0 second to make the turn at this pace + 2.0 seconds underwater.

**10.35 swimming + 3.0 seconds to make the turn and streamline underwater =**
**13.35 seconds per 25 yards =**
**26.7 seconds per 50 = 53.4 for the 100**

Shorter swimmers can approach the DPS figures of taller swimmers if we realize that *DPS is achieved by properly navigating the propulsive phases of the stroke.* With that in mind, there's no reason that my body can't move forward as far on a stroke as that of a taller swimmer. If we are affected to some degree by our height, and fall shy of the DPS numbers of some, then we can target a slightly faster rate of turnover to make up for the slightly shorter DPS.

Small swimmers, focus on DPS, not height.

## A 100-METER FREESTYLE COMPARISON:
## MARK SPITZ, 1972, AND NATHAN ADRIAN, 2012

Swimming times have gotten faster through the decades, and while we can take educated guesses as to why this is, the data behind the swims is concrete and helps us find the answer.

The following analysis compares the data behind Mark Spitz's 1972 Olympic gold medal 100 m freestyle swim in Munich with Nathan Adrian's gold medal swim in the same event 40 years later—London 2012.

| | **MARK SPITZ** | **NATHAN ADRIAN** |
|---|---|---|
| **EVENT** | 1972 Olympics 100-meter Freestyle | 2012 Olympics 100-meter Freestyle |
| **Time (sec.)** | 51.22 | 47.52 |
| **1st 50: Stroke Count and DPS** | 19.0 strokes (2.26 meters/stroke) | 16.5 strokes (2.36 meters/stroke) |
| **Start and Turn Data** | Surfaced at the 7 m mark off the start (underwater 2.5 seconds) | Surfaced at the 11 m mark off the start (underwater 3.4 seconds) |
| **2nd 50: Stroke Count and DPS** | 22.5 strokes (2.04 meters/stroke) | 19.0 strokes (2.26 meters/stroke) |
| **Start and Turn Data** | Surfaced at the 4 m mark (underwater 1.0 second) | Surfaced at the 7 m mark off the turn (underwater 2.5 seconds) |
| **Average Turnover Rate** | 1.10–1.15 seconds per stroke | 1.15–1.20 seconds per stroke |

Let's start by comparing their stroke counts on the first 50. There is a stark difference—Mark took 19 to Nathan's 16.5. From this one piece of data, we might surmise that technique/mechanics have changed dramatically. However, the stroke counts are not comparable due to the point at which each of these champion swimmers surfaced. If we look at the DPS of each (2.26 meters/stroke for Mark and 2.36 for Nathan), then we get a relevant comparison; however, DPS numbers are arbitrary for most of us in the sense that we don't know if a 0.1 difference in DPS is significant or not. Stroke counts are a much more relatable number. So, let's convert our data into comparable stroke count numbers, to which we can easily relate.

To generate a comparable stroke count number, we must note the time and distance spent underwater off the start and then use DPS to recalculate:

Nathan stayed underwater off the start to the 11 m mark. Mark stayed underwater to the 7 m mark.

If we tell Mark to abandon the pike dive of the 1970s and instead start like Nathan, and then we recalculate the number of strokes he takes on the first 50, based on his DPS, here is what we get:

If Mark surfaces at the 11 m mark and strokes with a DPS of 2.26 meters/ stroke (his DPS in Munich on the first 50), then his stroke count now becomes 17.2 strokes (39 meters divided by 2.26 meters/stroke). No swimmer actually takes 0.2 strokes, so let's round down to 17 strokes. We can even round up to 17.5 if we want. The point is, now compare the two stroke counts: Nathan was 16.5 strokes on the first 50. Mark is 17 or 17.5 now that he has a good start and surfaces at the 11 m mark where Nathan surfaced. The "stroke count" is not as big a difference as it appeared to be at first.

Let's do the same thing on the 2nd 50. Nathan surfaced at the 7 m mark off the turn. Mark surfaced at the 4 m mark. In our virtual game of swimming, we'll give Mark a good turn and have him surface at the 7 m mark. Applying his actual DPS of 2.04 meters/stroke from the 1972 race over a distance of 43 meters, we get a stroke count for Mark of 21.0 (43 meters divided by 2.04). It's not as close to Nathan's number as the first 50, but still the stroke count difference, when made relevant or "true," is a difference now of 2 full strokes (19 for Nathan and 21 for Mark) rather than the 3.5 stroke difference we observe in the race (19 for Nathan and 22.5 for Mark).

If we consider that Mark wore a nylon suit and dragged that ponderous mustache around, then can we make the leap to assume he would have been ½ stroke or 1 full stroke better? I can.

Keep in mind also that Mark turned over at a rate 0.05 faster per stroke cycle than Nathan. So, if we adjust Mark's start and turn to match Nathan as we just did, then the actual speed in the water (time spent swimming on the surface) compares as follows:

We'll insert the faster of the two rates for each swimmer. Mark turns over at 1.10–1.15, we'll plug the 1.10 into our example.

**1st 50 Mark: 17.5 strokes × 1.10 rate = 19.25 seconds**

Note that I calculated at 17.5 strokes instead of 17 strokes. If we give Mark a count of 17, then the time he spent swimming was 18.7 seconds.

Nathan turned over at a rate of 1.15 to 1.20, so we will plug in 1.15.

**1st 50 Nathan: 16.5 strokes × 1.15 rate = 18.97 seconds**

From the numbers can we say Mark was slower at swimming than Nathan? No, we can't, at least not on the first 50.

If we do the same on the 2nd 50, here is what we get:

**Mark: 21 strokes × 1.10 rate = 23.10 seconds**
**Nathan: 19 strokes × 1.15 rate = 21.85 seconds**

This is a 1.25-second difference on the 2nd 50. Nathan is notably faster.

So, there really is no difference in swimming time on the 1st 50 as shown in this analysis, but there is on the 2nd 50. It appears that today's swimmers maintain pace much better than swimmers did 40 years ago. This can be attributed to more sophisticated training, including strength training (stand Mark and Nathan side by side and you'll see David and Goliath).

The overall actual time difference in the 100 m performances is 3.70 seconds in the 40-year span between races. If 1.25 of that accounts for swimming on the 2nd 50, then we can say that 2.45 seconds is due to advanced starts, turns, and underwater speed. And if we make the leap that 1.25 seconds in swimming time is due to stronger swimmers and faster suits, then we can say that underwater freestyle propulsive pull path mechanics have not changed in 40 years.

# REFERENCES

Colwin, Cecil. 2002. *Breakthrough Swimming*. Champaign, IL: Human Kinetics.

Colwin, Cecil. 1999. *Swimming Dynamics*. Chicago: Masters Press.

Colwin, Cecil. 1992. *Swimming into the 21st Century*. Champaign, IL: Leisure Press.

Counsilman, James. 1994. *The New Science of Swimming*. Englewood Cliffs, NJ: Prentice-Hall.

Counsilman, James. 1968. *The Science of Swimming*. Englewood Cliffs, NJ: Prentice-Hall.

Crawford, Matthew B. 2009. *Shop Class as Soulcraft*. New York: Penguin Books.

Maglischo, Ernie. 2003. *Swimming Fastest*. Champaign, IL: Human Kinetics.

Maglischo, Ernie. 1982. *Swimming Faster*. Palo Alto, CA: Mayfield Publishing.

Weissmuller, Johnny. 1930. *Swimming the American Crawl*. London: Putnam.

# INDEX

*Note: Page numbers in boldface refer to figures and photographs.*

# ABOUT THE ATHLETES

## ELIZABETH BEISEL

2012 Olympic silver medalist in the 400 m IM,
2012 NCAA champion, 2011 world champion in the 400 IM

**BEST TIMES**
*400-yard IM: 3:58.84*
*400-meter IM (LCM): 4:31.27*

## JACK CONGER

2016 Olympic gold medalist in men's 4 × 200 m freestyle,
2017 bronze world champion in men's 4 × 200 m freestyle,
2015 NCAA champion

**BEST TIMES**
*200-meter freestyle: 1:45.77*
*100-meter freestyle: 49.02*
*50-meter freestyle: 22.69*

## ROWDY GAINES

10 world records set between 1978–84; 3 gold medals won at the 1984 Olympics; currently NBC's swimming commentator for the Olympics; masters swimming world record holder

**BEST TIMES**
*50-meter freestyle (LCM): 22.96 (1980)*
*100-meter freestyle (LCM): 49.36 (1981)*
*200-meter freestyle (LCM): 1:48.93 (1982)*

## TOWNLEY HAAS

2016 Olympic gold medalist in men's 4 × 200 m freestyle relay; US Open, American, NCAA, and Meet record holder in 200-yard freestyle; 2016 and 2017 NCAA champion in 200-yard freestyle

**BEST TIMES**
*200-meter freestyle: 1:45.03*
*100-meter freestyle: 48.20*
*50-meter freestyle 22.94*

## MARGARET KELLY

7-time NCAA All-American, 6-time Big Ten Champion

**BEST TIMES**
*500-yard freestyle: 4:48.63*
*200-yard freestyle: 1:48.88*
*100-yard freestyle: 49.12*

## ALLISON SCHMITT

2012 Olympic gold medalist, 2008 Olympic bronze medalist, world champion, NCAA champion

**BEST TIMES**
*400-meter freestyle: 4:01.77*
*200-meter freestyle: 1:53.61*

## PETER VANDERKAAY

3-time Olympian: 2004, 2008, and 2012;
5-time NCAA champion; 3-time world champion

**BEST TIMES**
*500-yard freestyle: 4:08.54*
*400-meter freestyle (LCM): 3:43.11*

## ASHLEY WHITNEY

1996 Olympic gold medalist in women's 4 × 200 m freestyle, 1999 NCAA champion, 2009 US Open Water champion

**BEST TIMES**
*800-meter freestyle: 8:36*
*400-meter freestyle: 4:13.46*
*200-meter freestyle (LCM): 2:00.43*

# ABOUT THE AUTHOR

At just over 5 foot 2 inches tall, and not having made her first Olympic team until the age of 27, Sheila Taormina seems an unlikely candidate to have competed in four consecutive summer olympiads in three completely different sports (swimming, 1996; triathlon, 2000 and 2004; and pentathlon, 2008). Her first two attempts to qualify for the Olympics in swimming (1988 and 1992)—during what were considered her "peak" years—came up short. Following those years, she moved forward with her education, finished her  master's degree in business in 1994, and then began a professional career in the automotive industry, working a full-time salaried position in Detroit.

With her eyes set on the possibilities of 1996, she trained before and after work with her small, hometown swim team in Livonia, Michigan. There were no corporate endorsements fueling the effort—just a plan, some hard work, and a coach who believed along with her. Sheila learned about technique, efficiency, and the keys to success. Applying those throughout the years, Sheila grew to become Olympic champion in one sport, world champion in a second sport, and the World Cup standings leader in a third sport.

In the end, Sheila Taormina experienced six different disciplines on the Olympic stage—swimming, cycling, running, pistol shooting, fencing, and equestrian show jumping. Her perspective on the Olympics, human potential, and performance is unparalleled.

Today Sheila travels extensively, from San Francisco to Bangkok to Johannesburg and everywhere in between, teaching the swim techniques from her book. She is also a popular corporate keynote speaker, relating the productivity and performance tools she used as an Olympic athlete to those of business executives across the globe.

Visit www.sheilat.com for more information.

# CREDITS

Art direction by Vicki Hopewell

Cover design by *the*BookDesigners

Interior design by Jessica Xavier

Photos by: Daniel Smith: pp. vii, xxiii, 15, 41 (frame 3), 47 (frames 1–4), 49 (frames 1–2), 68 (bottom frames), 81, 83, 85, 89, 92, 96, 103, 105, 111, 124, 130, 169 (Elizabeth Beisel), 170 (Rowdy Gaines), 171 (Ashley Whitney), 173; Brad Kaminski: p. 23; Kathy Coffin-Sheard: cover photo, pp. 37 (frames 4–6), 39, 41 (frame 4), 42, 43, 45, 47 (frames 5–8), 49 (frame 4), 51–55, 57 (frame 1), 59–62, 64–67, 69 (bottom frames), 75–80, 82, 84, 86, 87, 90, 93, 98, 107, 109, 113, 115, 117, 119, 121, 122, 126 (top right, bottom right), 128 (top right, bottom right), 135; Michelle Taylor-McCraw: pp. 125, 126 (top left, bottom left), 128 (top left, bottom left), 129

Illustrations by Nicole Kaufman

Reprinted with permission of the International Swimming Hall of Fame: p. xx (Johnny Weissmuller); reprinted with permission of Indiana University, The Counsilman Center for the Science of Swimming: pp. 43, 49, 68, 69 (Mike Troy and Mark Spitz); reprinted with permission of USA Swimming: pp. 169 (Jack Conger), 170 (Townley Haas), 171 (Allison Schmitt and Peter Vanderkaay); reprinted with permission of University of Michigan Photography: p. 170 (Margaret Kelly)

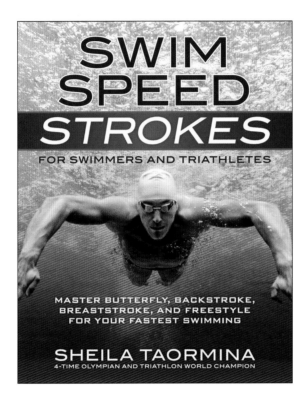